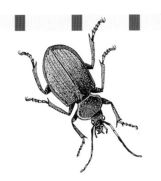

A Beginner's Field Guide

WATCHING NATURE

Monica Russo

Photographs by Kevin Byron

Sterling Publishing Co., Inc. New York

This book is dedicated to my mom and dad,
intuitive experts in growing the flowers, trees, and shrubs that attract wildlife.

Edited by Jeanette Green
Designed by Judy Morgan

Library of Congress Cataloging-in-Publication Data

Russo, Monica.
Watching nature: a beginner's field guide / Monica Russo:
photographs by Kevin Byron.
    p. cm.
   Includes index.
   Summary: Describes how to make close-up observations of nature and
how to record what you see, including recognizing field marks,
identifying plants, noting characteristic sounds, and watching
specific animal activities.
   1. Wildlife watching—Juvenile literature. 2. Nature study—
Juvenile literature. [1. Wildlife watching. 2. Nature study.]
I. Byron, Kevin, ill. II. Title.
QL60.R87 1998
508—dc21
                                                           97-51572

1 3 5 7 9 10 8 6 4 2
First paperback edition published in 2002 by
Sterling Publishing Company, Inc.
387 Park Avenue South, New York, N.Y. 10016
© 1998 by Monica Russo
Distributed in Canada by Sterling Publishing
c/o Canadian Manda Group, One Atlantic Avenue, Suite 105
Toronto, Ontario, Canada M6K 3E7
Distributed in Australia by Capricorn Link (Australia) Pty Ltd.
P.O. Box 704, Windsor, NSW 2756 Australia
Printed in China
All rights reserved

Sterling ISBN 0-8069-9515-7 Hardcover
ISBN 1-4027-0130-6 Paperback

READER'S CAUTION

The outdoor world can be dangerous. Many different types of animals can bite; some are venomous. The sting from a single honeybee can be lethal to some individuals. And many ticks in the United States carry Lyme disease. Even plants may cause a severe allergic reaction. Readers who enjoy the outdoors do so at their own risk and should take responsible precautions. Parental guidance is suggested for many outdoor activities.

CONTENTS

ACKNOWLEDGMENTS

Despite decades of field work, a naturalist may have the opportunity to observe rare or endangered species only a few times. Those opportunities are increased when you can visit a variety of habitats. We would like to thank the Strauchen family and the Legros family for providing the opportunity and luxury to observe beyond our usual territory.

Many friends and professionals have helped and encouraged us over the years, especially Professor Heinz Meng at the State University of New York at New Paltz and the entomologists from the Insect & Disease Lab at Augusta, Maine. Our sincere appreciation also goes to expert gardeners Jane and Dick and to the neighbors and friends who brought specimens or data to our attention. We also thank Tri-Town Publishing in Dover, New Hampshire, for permission to reprint several of Kevin's black-and-white prints.

Finally, our thanks to our editor, Jeanette Green, at Sterling Publishing, who guided us in designing a book that will help others more closely observe and appreciate the natural world.

—MONICA RUSSO and KEVIN BYRON

American copper butterfly.

INTRODUCTION

From birdwatching in your own backyard to taking a whale-watch cruise, this book will increase your enjoyment of nature. Whether you're working in a garden, relaxing on vacation, or hiking and camping, you'll discover how to develop your observation skills. And you'll make a lasting personal record of everything you've seen.

This book has been designed to show beginners how to:

- look for clues to animal activities
- remember bird songs
- attract birds, butterflies, and other wildlife to your backyard
- develop the skills needed to identify wildflowers
- look for distinctive field marks on wildlife
- keep an accurate journal of your outdoor discoveries
- make on-the-spot field sketches and take outdoor photos

This is not a complicated field guide or a technical manual, so you don't need to worry about scientific words and classifications. It's designed to help all beginning naturalists, young and old, to get the most from outdoor experiences and to create a lasting record of observations.

A freshly emerged black swallowtail butterfly rests and dries its wings.

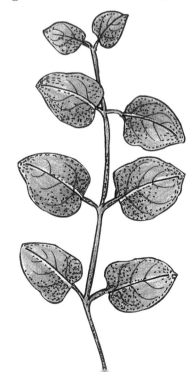

WILDLIFE WATCHING

How Do They Do It?

Have you ever wondered how birdwatchers and naturalists get just a fleeting glimpse of an animal and then identify it confidently? They do it by looking for specific field marks. A *field mark* is any color or pattern that identifies an animal as a member of a particular group or as a single species. Think of a field mark as a trademark, emblem, or hallmark of an animal.

Stripes on a small mammal's back are easy field marks to look for. This is an eastern chipmunk from North America.

Field marks are usually easy to see from a distance or while using binoculars. Look for these colors and patterns while watching an animal "in the field" (in its natural habitat).

Here are some examples of field marks on mammals.

stripes, spots, or streaks

bands or rings around the tail

mask: a dark band across the face or around the eyes

large claws to dig or climb with

Field Marks on Birds

Many birds have such complicated patterns that it's sometimes difficult to remember them. Here are some field marks to look for on birds.

bars or bands across the tail

narrow bar of white across the wing (wing-bar)

eye-ring: a white or colored ring around the eye

➤ eyebrow: a streak of contrasting color above the eye

➤ bib: dark area under the throat

➤ white throat

➤ neck bands, rings, or a "necklace" (a broken band)

➤ spots: these might be large round spots, or fine speckles

➤ crest or long head feathers

The crest and black "chinstrap" on this North American blue jay are prominent field marks.

The two black bands on the front of this killdeer are obvious field marks. Other shorebird species have neck bands also.

The Shape of Things

The overall shape or profile of a bird is important. Is it slender, chunky, short-tailed, big-headed? Kingfishers, a group of birds composed of several families, have big heads and sword-shaped bills, whether it's a kingfisher in North America, Great Britain, Australia, or Europe. Nuthatches are small birds with short, squarish tails and very

short necks. These birds live in North America, Great Britain, and Europe; the closely related sitellas of Australia are very similar.

Measuring Up

You can probably already identify some common birds in your neighborhood: house sparrows, ducks, geese, or city pigeons. Use these familiar birds as measuring guides when trying to judge the size of a *wild* bird.

Most kingfishers have a big-headed, sword-billed appearance in silhouette. This is a belted kingfisher from North America.

The Right Moves

A bird's movements, behavior, or posture can be the give-away trademark of a particular species. Here are some examples.

The spotted sandpiper of Canada and the United States bobs its tail up and down constantly.

In Great Britain and Europe, several species of wagtail tip their tails up and down repeatedly. They have long tails, so this is easy to see.

In northern and eastern Australia, the rufous fantail swishes its tail from side to side as it hunts for insects in the trees. The tail movements may help to stir up a quick meal.

Don't forget to look at how a bird walks: pigeons and doves walk along the ground, but other birds may take short hops. Some birds can run smoothly and quickly, while others stalk their prey slowly and carefully.

Look for head stripes or "eyelines" across the side of the face when you're out birdwatching. This is a red-breasted nuthatch from North America. Nuthatches in Great Britain and Europe are similar.

Butterflies, Moths, Beetles, and Other Insects

When you're looking for field marks on insects, try to get a good look at these:

 the shape or length of the antennae

 wing patterns: borders, bands, or stripes

 camouflage: patterns or colors that mimic tree bark, leaves, or lichens

 *eye spots (false eyes):* large round spots that may serve to frighten away predators

Some field marks are so unique that they become the basis for the insect's name. The buckeye butterfly of North America is named for its large, round eyespots.

The long, graceful antennae of this beetle help classify it as a member of the longhorn family.

Field marks on butterflies include stripes, spots, or wide bands of color. The white bands on this butterfly identify it as a North American white admiral.

Many insects have "eye-spots," or false eyes, which may confuse or startle predators. Many butterfly, moth, and beetle species have large or colorful eye-spots. This is a North American pearly-eye.

Reptiles and Amphibians

Look for simple, obvious field marks: stripes, bands, or spots. You can get quite close to frogs, toads, salamanders, and land turtles to see field marks. You can even try taking photographs or making a field sketch. Some water turtles, how-ever, will slide right off into the water as soon as you approach. You may have to observe them from a distance with binoculars. Many lizards also are sensitive to nearby movements and just speed away as soon as you get close!

People often report snakes to be much larger than they really are. Hikers may be so startled by an encounter with a snake that they remember it as larger than life. Try using something familiar to judge the length of a snake accurately. Is it half as long as your hiking stick? As long as the edge of your trail map? You *don't* need to get close, you just need to make a calm, realistic estimate.

Some species of snake are venomous. If you live in an area where poisonous snakes are common, make an effort to learn what they look like and where they live. Visit a local nature center or museum; they may have living specimens on exhibit. Remember: You NEVER have to get close to any animal. You can watch it through binoculars, or you can just walk away quietly, if you feel worried.

A dark mask is an obvious field mark on some animals. This is a wood frog, a common amphibian in much of Canada and the northeastern United States.

You Do It All the Time

Every time you meet a new friend or classmate, you automatically take note of many details: the person's tone of voice, gait, gestures, and style of clothes or shoes chosen to wear. You may meet someone who is restless and fidgety or someone who is quiet and calm. You could probably identify a friend or relative by voice or by how he or she steps when entering a room, even if your eyes are closed!

This black-capped chickadee of North America has a black cap and "bib" as its identifying field marks. In Great Britain and much of Europe, the marsh tit and willow tit are quite similar in appearance and are closely related to the chickadee.

Use these natural observation skills to remember the field marks and behavior of birds, butterflies, mammals, or frogs. Your ability to notice details of color, pattern, and movement will improve as you spend more time in the field.

Did You Know . . . ?

The color of your clothes isn't important for most bird-watching activities. Birds have excellent color vision, but they are also extremely alert to movement and sounds. They are likely to see you, no matter *what* you're wearing!

Special Effects

Different outdoor conditions may affect how well you see animals. Here are some examples.

Bright sunlight can make an animal appear lighter in color.

A glare can conceal a field mark.

A dark area seen on a bird may actually be a shadow.

Mist, fog, and rain can obscure details. And if you are wet and uncomfortable, you're not likely to take time to look for important details.

The season and even the age or gender of an animal may make identification difficult. Here are some examples.

In North America, most birds molt their feathers during the year. They may look entirely different in the spring, compared to winter.

The male red kangaroo of Australia's grassland is indeed reddish in color. But the female 'roos are distinctly blue-gray.

Bald eagles in North America are dark brown as young birds. They don't get a solid white head and tail until they are five to six years old!

On the Move

Now that you know *what* to look for, what's the best way to observe wildlife? Should you sit still or go out and search? Sometimes the best way to watch an animal is to slowly and quietly follow it at a distance. Small mammals such as squirrels

Observing small mammals while they eat gives you a better chance to see details—such as the white eye-rings on this North American red squirrel.

have a small home territory, so you don't need to cover much ground to observe them. A woodchuck in a clover field or a hedgehog in an English garden is a good choice if you want to try this.

Birds, of course, can simply fly away. Try walking closer and closer, smoothly and quietly. Don't make any movements with your arms or hands. Even raising a camera or binoculars to your eyes will scare off a bird. Try not to walk directly toward a bird—walk in a big half-circle around the bird as it feeds. A bird is very likely to see you as you approach, but it may stay where it is for a longer time if you are slow, careful, and quiet.

Starting Small

Slow, quiet stalking is especially useful for observing insects. You can watch a large beetle hunting in the leaf litter for prey or digging in the ground. You can watch most sand wasps and

digger wasps closely as they dig in the sand to construct a nursery. You may even see one fly in with prey to store in her burrow for her expected young. And you will be able to observe butterflies in almost any garden as they drink nectar from flowers.

The tiger stripes on this large butterfly help identify it as an eastern tiger swallowtail of North America. Different species of swallowtail, sometimes called Papilios, are found in Great Britain, Europe, and Australia.

Many insects react immediately to shadows and movement nearby. A butterfly feeding at flowers in bright sunlight may fly away as soon as your shadow covers it. Some beetles just fold up their legs and fall from the leaves to the ground below, disappearing before you have a good chance to get close or take a photograph. So before you walk up to flowers or foliage too closely, scan the blossoms and the leaf surfaces quickly to see what's there.

Have a Seat!

Brisk, vigorous hiking along a woodland trail is excellent for your health, but you probably won't see much wildlife if you're bustling along. Slow down and settle yourself on a rock or log. Most large parks even have benches, observation blinds, or decks built along the trails. If your goal is to finish a particular trail for a sense of accomplishment or to exercise for a specific amount of time, you won't be able to fully appreciate the natural world around you until that goal is met. Wait until you've done your mile; then take some time out to watch wildlife.

Many experienced birdwatchers don't even get out of their cars to go birding! They just find a favorite spot near a pond, field, or weedy hedgerow, park the car, and roll down the window to watch birds. Cars hide most of your body and your arm movements. With the window down, the door can support your arms steadily while you hold a camera or binoculars. The only drawback may be a strained back or neck from remaining in one position too long. Switch to opposite sides of the car, or take a break to avoid any aches and pains!

Three's a Crowd

If you are with a friend, it may be hard to sit still and not talk. But there can be advantages to watching wildlife in small groups.

You can all face different directions. The more alert your observers are, the more you all may see!

You can compare your observations with those of your friends to be sure that everyone has seen the same field marks or behavior.

Groups of people often attract opportunistic animals. For example, squirrels in North America wait at park benches for handouts. And gulls around the world swoop to steal food from beach-goers—whether you're on the sandy beaches of Australia, the rocky coast of Maine, or the grassy cliffs of Great Britain!

Most parks and nature reservations have strict regulations against feeding wild animals. Human food is *not* usually appropriate for wildlife, and it may even be harmful. One example is bread and doughnuts thrown out to birds during the winter. These foods do not have the calories or nutritional value a bird needs when it is going to spend the night at below-zero

Take time to sit down, look, and listen for wildlife. Most parks and large sanctuaries, like this one in Campobello Island in New Brunswick, Canada, have benches or observation decks for wildlife watchers.

temperatures! Food may also attract undesirable species, such as rats, or dangerous species, such as bears.

What's Going On Here?

On your hikes outdoors, or while working in your garden, you are likely to observe a variety of wildlife activities. How many of these behaviors have you already noticed?

Self-Care Activities bathing, grooming and preening; resting or sleeping; eating; drinking; storing or hiding food

Home Life attracting mates (courting, singing); mating; nest-building; feeding mates or young

Behavior in Groups and Interactions with Other Animals hunting or killing prey; defense of territory; group vocalizing (howling,

singing, etc.); group feeding (mammals grazing, butterflies at puddles); resting or sleeping in groups; migrations in groups; signaling or alerting others to danger

You will quickly find that some of these activities are common, while others are a challenge to wait for.

Is This Really Happening?

Watching a lizard drink water is a simple and unquestionable observation. It is probably hot and dry, and the animal needs water. But other activities may not be so clear! Here are a few examples.

A pair of butterflies swirl around each other in flight. It looks like a courtship display. But maybe not: the two butterflies may both be males, engaged in an intense territorial battle! Many butterfly species pugnaciously defend their home territory.

In North America, a blue jay flies off from a feeding station with a chunk of beef suet. Will it eat the suet once it lands? Not always. During the winter, a blue jay might tuck the suet into the snow or leaves at the base of a tree and actually cover it, creating a food cache it can come back to.

A large, digger wasp emerges from her burrow (an underground nursery dug in sandy soil). The female wasp carefully covers up the entrance hole with tiny pebbles and then flies off. Is the nursery complete and her work done? Not at all! She has just gone out hunting

A bird-feeding station provides an opportunity to observe field marks while birds are eating. Note the reddish cap and white wing-bar on this common redpoll, a species found in North America, Great Britain, and parts of Europe.

Shorebirds usually migrate in flocks. During migration, they can be observed feeding in groups, and resting together.

for caterpillars and will return later to stock the nursery with prey. She will dig out the entrance hole again and drag a captured caterpillar down into the burrow. When she leaves, perhaps for the last time, she will once again carefully camouflage the entrance hole.

It's Professional

Your outdoor experiences and observations are mostly for personal pleasure. For some people, however, wildlife watching is a serious occupation. Biologists, entomologists, herpetologists,

and many other scientists are all likely to make detailed studies of animal activities. To all these professionals, direct observation and clear, accurate field notes are very important. See chapter 8, The Naturalist's Notebook, for suggestions about keeping a journal of your own outdoor observations.

chapter two

LANDMARKS & HIGHLIGHTS

Trailside Landmarks

Along any trail or path you're sure to notice large natural landmarks, like a big, mossy stump or a fallen tree with its roots exposed. Some landmarks, however, may be constructed by humans, such as a stone wall, old fence posts, a footbridge, or a causeway. All these landmarks can help you remember where you've made particular observations, and you may want to write about them in your outdoor notebook. They can also help you remember the design of a trail system, especially one that you hike frequently.

Another reason to be alert to landmarks is that animals are also aware of them as highlights in their own territory. A squirrel or other small mammal may consistently use the same stump to nibble on seeds or to clean and groom its fur. Small mammals often climb onto fence posts or tall stumps to get a better look at their neighborhood. Birds use fence posts, large fallen branches, or bare overhanging branches to sing or call from. A standing dead tree (a "snag") with fungus and peeling bark attracts insects, so it will also be a feeding site for birds. Hollow logs and

A pine snag with peeling bark makes an excellent home for birds, small mammals, and insects.

Squirrels, chipmunks, and other small mammals often leave obvious evidence of their mealtimes.

This partially uprooted pine creates a perfect den or hiding place for small animals.

hollow snags become the homes to many mammal, bird, and insect species.

So, the landmarks that seem interesting to you are also likely to be very important to wildlife!

Smaller Clues

Whenever you pass through a dense stand of evergreen trees, inspect the ground for small clues to wildlife activity. In most woodlands or forested areas around the world, hawks and owls use older larger trees for roosting and nesting. Look carefully on the ground under these big trees, and you may be lucky enough to find a casting. A *casting* is a compact, compressed pellet of fur and bones that has been regurgitated by a hawk or owl, hours after it has eaten a meal. The meat of the prey has been digested,

These castings from an owl, partly disintegrated by rain, clearly show the skulls and bones of rodents it has eaten.

but the fur, bones, and even teeth are compacted together inside the bird's crop—an area above the stomach—and then regurgitated by mouth. Hawk castings usually have a great amount of fur or feathers, while owl castings contain many more bones and even the teeth of its prey. A small falcon that has been eating crickets and beetles will produce a casting composed of the hard parts of those insects, such as the wings and legs.

Biologists and ornithologists can often identify exactly what a hawk, falcon, or owl has eaten by carefully taking apart a casting. They can identify mammals by their teeth and small birds by their skulls. Observe closely, but be careful.

This is the skull of a North American raccoon, weathered and bleached by rain and sun, and cleaned by insects.

Many people easily confuse a bird's casting with the excrement (feces) of a fox or other predatory mammal, since there may be fur or feathers included. These mammalian droppings would be dangerous to handle because they contain harmful bacteria and other organisms.

Along any wilderness trail you may find the skull or bones of a wild animal, since these animals usually die in their natural habitats. But unfortunately, many wild creatures are killed by domestic dogs and cats, and dragged some distance. So, you may find the remains of wildlife where you least expect it!

Among the Rocks

Some unique trail-side landmarks may include rocky slopes, stone walls, a ridge of exposed ledge rock, or a jumble of boulders. A rock pile can be a haven for many types of wildlife. In hot, dry climates, a loose jumble of rocks may attract lizards and snakes seeking cool shade. Rocky slopes and stone walls are perfect hiding places for small mammals, too. Birds may also hunt along the rocks for spiders and insects. Before you approach any rocky landmark, scan the surface first with binoculars to see what might be there.

Diggers and Dusters

Many animal species around the world dig and scratch in the ground for food. You can find evidence of digging animals in almost any habitat: open fields, shady woodlands, desert areas, or even your own garden. Some animals are looking for insect larvae, such as beetle grubs, while others are trying to dig up roots and tubers to eat. Some mammals even dig up underground wasp nests to eat the nutritious wasp larvae, leaving pieces of the nest and comb scattered all around. Finding evidence of digging along a well-used trail or in your backyard proves that wildlife is active in the area.

You may also notice bare areas of dry, dusty dirt used by birds for taking dust baths. Birds scratch aside surface pebbles and debris and may even scratch out a shallow bowllike depression, which becomes a favorite spot to dust-bathe, especially in hot weather.

A North American wood-pecker, the yellow-bellied sapsucker, has made the holes in this pine bark.

It looks like an anthill, but this is the entrance to the nest of a digger wasp.

Here is the entrance of an eastern chipmunk's burrow, made at the base of a moss-covered stump.

Holes and Hideaways

Some of the most interesting clues to animal activity are holes. Small holes in tree bark or in dead snags may be made by birds seeking insects. The smallest holes may be made by the insects themselves. Tiny holes in large seeds, such as acorns, are made when an insect inside has matured and must gnaw its way out.

Small holes in sand or fine dirt, found in the open sun along trails, may be the nests of digger wasps. These insects make individual nests instead of large hives. Several females may dig nurseries together in a loose colony, so you may find eight or ten holes near each other. Each entrance hole may be barely the diameter of a pencil and surrounded by a mound of fine dirt.

Stop and watch to see if a mother wasp returns to her nursery, carrying prey for her expected young.

Larger holes in the ground are made by small mammals. In North America mice, voles, moles, shrews, chipmunks, and ground squirrels all live in underground dens made in loose dirt, under leaves, or beneath soft moss. These holes may later be used by other animals: toads, snakes, and even wintering bumblebees often live in old mammal tunnels.

Of course, large mammals, like foxes, bears, and skunks, use large burrows. However, they are not as likely to choose a den site very close to a trail. You may see paths or runways worn through tall grasses. In North America these may be made by deer, woodchucks, rabbits, or hare.

Tracks

Animal tracks provide obvious clues to wildlife activity. But finding good, clear tracks is not easy. The surface sand or dirt must be flat, smooth, and free of leaves and debris to see tracks clearly. Tracks "age." The fine edges become worn by wind or rain, and tiny grains of sand settle. Freshly made imprints are the best to study. Look along the edge of a pond or river, along sandy or dusty roadsides, or in the loose, soft dirt of your garden.

This hoofprint of a white-tailed deer was made in soft dirt along a country road.

Try this: Find a flat area where there is loose, soft dirt. Rake it smooth and use your hands to brush it clean. Observe this test area daily for several days to see if you have any regular visitors. Watch for the tracks of common, well-known animals—even domestic dogs and cats. You'll be able to recognize their tracks in a short time, and then you won't confuse them with those of other animals.

Cocoon and Chrysalis Hunt

At the end of summer or during winter, you may find a cocoon or a chrysalis. A cocoon is a sort of safety envelope that a larva makes with silk. Inside, the larva sheds its skin and becomes a pupa. It will later emerge from the cocoon as a moth. Most cocoons look fuzzy or fibrous.

A chrysalis is a pupa, too, but it will develop into a butterfly. A chrysalis is usually smooth, and it may have colorful dots, spots, or spines on it. Cocoons and chrysalises are usually firmly attached to twigs or stems with silk, but many cocoons are also formed on the ground. You're likely to find a cocoon or chrysalis on:

🦋 the stems of small shrubs or tall woody weeds

🦋 the stalks of plants in your garden, late in the season

Inside this large cocoon, the pupa will develop into a beautiful cecropia moth.

🦋 under your house eaves or behind shutters

🦋 wedged under loose bark or inside the deep crevices of a tree trunk

IIIIIIIIII *A cecropia moth, freshly emerged from its cocoon, hangs from a branch to dry its wings. The cecropia belongs to the giant silk-moth family and is native to eastern North America.*

IIIIIIIIII *A thin strand of silk helps keep this chrysalis attached upright to a plant stem. It will soon develop into a black swallowtail butterfly.*

Finding a chrysalis or cocoon is evidence that the larva (a caterpillar) had been eating a plant which only that particular species is attracted to. A stand of wildflowers may be nearby, which you should investigate during the next flowering season to look for butterflies feeding or laying eggs. You can also return to check on the cocoon or chrysalis to see if the adult insect has successfully emerged, leaving behind an empty outer husk.

IIIIIIIIII *This colorful, spotted chrysalis hangs head-downward, attached with silk to the twig. After just a few weeks, a Baltimore butterfly will emerge from the chrysalis.*

Feathers on the Ground

As you spend more time outdoors, you are more likely to find the molted feathers of birds. All birds have to grow new feathers as old plumage becomes worn or damaged. The old feathers drop out and are replaced by new ones. Molted feathers can be found in the forest, on the beach, on a city sidewalk, along a roadside, or near a feeding station. A biologist, ornithologist, or experienced birdwatcher can often deter-

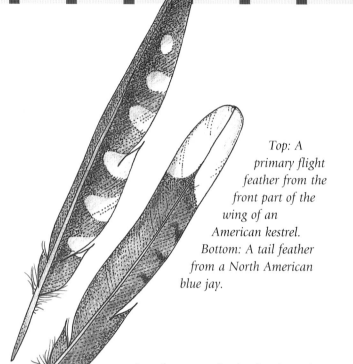

Top: A primary flight feather from the front part of the wing of an American kestrel. Bottom: A tail feather from a North American blue jay.

mine from a single feather the species of bird, the gender and age of the bird, and even the general health of the individual bird.

Feathers with a wide vane on each side of the quill are usually tail feathers. Feathers with a narrow vane along one side of the quill are probably *primaries*, the primary flight feathers from the front part of the wing. These feathers are usually gracefully tapered. Smaller, soft, curved feathers are from the body. The condition of the feather itself shows the wear and tear that daily life imposes on a wild bird. You may see ragged, worn edges. Pieces may actually be missing or torn away. There may even be faint stress marks—lines across the vane and quill—that have weakened the strength of the feather. These are the result of physical stress, such as reduced food supply.

Several feathers found on the ground together may be evidence that a hawk or owl has killed a smaller bird and plucked some of its feathers out.

The molted tail feather of a pigeon found on a city sidewalk. You can find molted feathers in almost any habitat.

Insect Wings

The wings of large insects, such as beetles, moths, butterflies, or dragonflies, are sometimes found on the ground. You may find them along a roadside or trail or in your garden or driveway. These severed wings, or pieces of wings, are the remains of a bird's meal or a toad's dinner. Insect-eating birds often catch large insects in flight and then snap off the hard, tough wings. A small foraging mammal may find a beetle, munch away the softer parts for a meal, and then discard the harder parts. Toads also may snap up a moth at night and leave the large wings behind. These severed wings are excellent clues to the presence and feeding habits of small wildlife in your area.

The hind wings of an Io moth are all that remains of a bird's meal.

chapter three

FLOWERS, TREES & LICHENS

Food and Shelter

Wherever you live on earth, plants provide food and shelter for wildlife. Here are some examples.

Flowers attract colorful butterflies, moths, bees, beetles, hover flies, and digger wasps. All these insects feed on the nectar or pollen from flowers, and many also pollinate plants.

Tiny predators, such as crab spiders and ambush bugs, hide among flowers. They catch and eat any small insects that land on the same flower.

In North America, hummingbirds feed on the nectar from flowers such as lobelias, mints, and honeysuckle.

Bayberry shrubs in the eastern United States provide berries for birds all winter long. A colony of bayberry shrubs may be the best place to observe yellow-rumped warblers during the winter.

A stand of pines is a good place to look for birds that feed on the small seeds inside cones. Crossbills in Great Britain, Europe, and North America have sharp,

Wildflowers in fields and woodlands attract butterflies, bees, wasps, and other pollinating insects.

curved tips on their bills which help them pry out pine seeds from cones.

Oak trees always attract mammals. Oak acorns provide food for many species of large and small mammals. Many birds eat acorns, too.

Hawthorns and other spiny, thorny, or prickly trees and shrubs provide excellent nesting sites and cover for *songbirds* around the world.

A crab spider waits to ambush any small insect that lands on the flower. These well-camouflaged spiders are found in North America, Great Britain, and Australia.

Just Read the Label!

Most people enjoy the beauty of wildflowers, even if they can't identify them. But once you start looking at wildflowers on your hikes, you'll probably want to learn just what they are! Here are some ideas to help you out.

Always look at a trail guide when visiting a park system or natural area. Many describe numbered sites with signs and show pictures of the plants or flowers at each site.

Ask a staff naturalist or park ranger what wildflower species are in bloom and where to look for them. They are often happy to show you where to find favorite wildflowers.

Many public gardens and arboretums have trails with labeled wildflowers and flowering shrubs. There may also be a walking guide to the plants along each path. Take advantage of good trails with labeled plants. It's an excellent way to learn the names of flowers and shrubs.

Look for an organized, group wildflower walk or garden tour in your area. These walks, given by botanists and trained naturalists, are scheduled during peak blooming times.

In a public sanctuary or wildflower garden, orchids are likely to be labeled or identified in a trail guide. This lady-slipper orchid is native to eastern North America.

This red trillium is an early spring wildflower seen in New England woodlands. Several species of trillium are found in North America and Great Britain.

Some species of aster have so many petals that you wouldn't want to count them! Along with daisies, dandelions, and thistles, asters are members of the Composite family.

Coltsfoot flowers bloom early in the spring in wet areas. They are native to Great Britain but have been naturalized in North America.

Out on Your Own

While you are out hiking or camping, you may notice wildflowers that you'd like to identify, but you don't have a botanical field guide or don't know how to use one. Sometimes a park naturalist can identify them for you, by your description. However, many different plants are very similar to each other. That's why your description must be very accurate. Simply telling a botanist that you saw a yellow flower with lots of small leaves is *not* enough information for identification.

Here are some observations that can help you to accurately describe a flower or to identify it in a trail guide.

Judge how high from the ground the flower is. Is it about knee-high or right near the ground?

Count how many separate petals are on the flower. Are there just four, for example, or so many that you don't really want to count them? Members of the mustard family (cabbage family) around the world all have four petals. But dandelions and many species of aster have flowers with so many thin petals you'd never want to count them.

Is the flower really a sort of trumpet or tube shape without any separate petals?

What kind of colors or patterns are on

The three green sepals on this painted trillium are easy to distinguish from the three white petals.

the flower? Are there stripes, dots, spots? Is the center a different color?

Look for the sepals; they usually look like a set of green petals. Are they longer than the petals?

It sounds like a lot of details to look for, but these close-up, accurate observations are needed to identify the plant. Details of shape, color, texture, size, and patterns are all important, because many different plant species look similar.

Create Your Own Image

Use your field notebook or sketchbook to make a drawing of the flower or to write your observations in, so you can remember exactly what it looked like. You'll be able to describe it more accurately to a park naturalist later. If you are hiking in an area where there are many new wildflowers you haven't seen before, a notebook or sketchbook will help you keep track of all the different plants you've seen.

You don't need to be an accomplished artist to make a field sketch. Just draw anything that will help you to remember the details of the flower clearly and accurately. For example, you can show just how long a leaf or petal is. Write notes about the coloring or make a rough drawing showing how large an individual flower is. These are your own private drawings, and an art teacher won't be looking at them.

Looking at Leaves

Although a flower may be the most beautiful and memorable finding on an outdoor walk, noticing the details on leaves is just as important. Observing the shape and arrangement of leaves on a stem helps a good deal in identifying plants. Here are some observations you can easily make.

The leaves of some wildflowers grow only at the base of the stem. This is called a *rosette* of leaves. The common dandelion has leaves arranged in a rosette.

The leaves of many plants grow in a rosette at the base of the stem.

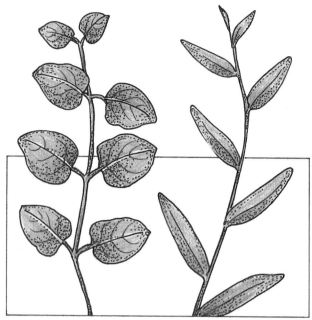

Leaves may be arranged in pairs opposite each other (left), or they may be alternate, staggered along the stem (right).

Ajuga, a member of the mint family, has paired leaves. Native to Great Britain, it is widely planted in the United States as a groundcover for landscaping.

Leaves may be arranged in *pairs* on the stem—directly *opposite* each other. Plants in the mint family, including garden sage, catnip, and peppermint, have opposite, paired leaves.

Leaves can be attached *alternately,* or staggered—not in pairs.

Estimate the overall size of each leaf. Is it as long as your thumb or thumbnail? As wide across as your palm?

Is the edge of the leaf smooth? Wavy? Is there a "sawtooth" edge?

Does the leaf have a notable texture? Leaves may be waxy, leathery, thick, fuzzy, smooth, or rough.

All these observations can help you identify a wildflower or shrub in a trail guide or describe it to a naturalist. And even if you don't care to identify individual plants, it's helpful to notice these details for other reasons.

The veins of these orchid leaves grow in parallel rows. But many other plant species have leaf veins which fan out or are finely webbed.

You can compose a better photograph of a wildflower, so the most interesting details will be included.

You'll notice fine details more easily when you want to make a good field drawing.

Sharpening your observation skills is helpful for all wildlife watchers and birdwatchers.

You can let other hikers know where wildflowers are along the trail. No one should miss out on a beautiful group of flowers!

No one should pass by a beauty like this purple-flowering raspberry. Always let other hikers know where to see interesting wildflowers along the trail.

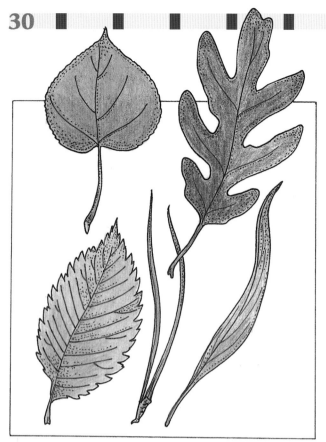

Observing leaf shape and size is easy. Leaves may be rounded or heart-shaped, like this quaking aspen (top left), or have the fingerlike lobes of a white oak (top right). On the bottom left is an elm leaf with a typical sawtooth edge. The long, thin needles of a Scotch pine (middle) grow in twos. On the right is the narrow, graceful leaf of a eucalyptus.

Just Trees

Most trees and large shrubs are identified easily by their leaves. If you are visiting a large park or reserve, there may be a guide to the trees found there. Be sure to look at the guide before you set out on the trail, so you know what to look for.

Use the same observation skills for noticing the details on tree leaves as you have used for the leaves of wildflowers. Look at shape, size, and texture. Inspect the trees planted around your neighborhood school, shopping center, or town streets, so you can practice noticing details. If you positively know just one kind of tree—a cultivated apple, for example—you can use it as a comparison. You'll be able to remember whether another leaf is bigger, smaller, rougher, or smoother than the apple leaves you are familiar with.

Every autumn tour buses give leaf-watchers a chance to view the brilliant foliage on New England's sugar maples.

Ornamental and Exotic Trees

Trees and flowering shrubs that grow near houses and public buildings and along city streets and highways are probably not wild, native trees at all. They are probably *ornamentals,* or exotic species, grown in a nursery and used for landscaping or in gardens. The trees and shrubs may actually be native and wild to a completely different continent. But they have successfully adapted and acclimated to a new environment, and may thrive in your region. Here are some examples.

Seed pods from Australian eucalyptus trees. Each species of eucalyptus (gum) tree has different types of pods.

If you live in California, you may see several species of eucalyptus (gum) tree. They are native to Australia, where there are over 500 species of wild eucalyptus tree.

The European rowan tree is widely planted in North America, where it is called the European mountain ash. It is not a member of the ash family at all; it belongs to the rose family, along with apples and hawthorns.

The earleaf acacia of Florida is actually a native of New South Wales in Australia. Acacia trees are often called wattles in Australia. There are hundreds of different species.

North American tree farmers who grow plantations of "Christmas trees" often grow Scotch pines, an evergreen that's native and wild in Great Britain and Europe.

Hands Off!

In North America, poison ivy and poison sumac plants should be avoided. Even the slightest brush against their leaves can cause a severe, itching, burning rash that may last for days! In North America and Great Britain, the stinging nettle can also cause a stinging, burning reaction.

Wherever you live, learn about the plants in your area that are dangerous to touch. Ask an experienced gardener, forester, naturalist, or park ranger to show you where these plants can be found.

Not Just Leaves

The texture and color of bark on a trunk can be important in identifying a tree. The common beech of Great Britain and the American beech (different species) both have smooth, gray bark. The American sycamore normally has patchy, flaky bark. And the stringybark gum of Australia is named for its long loose, fibrous strips of bark.

You may also notice unusual buds, thorns, spines, seed cones, or pods on twigs and branches. All these details can help you to match up a picture in a trail guide or park poster with the tree you have seen.

Don't be afraid to ask park rangers or naturalists to help you identify a tree. Most of them enjoy talking about their favorite species! Local foresters, nursery workers, and agricultural agents may also be able to help you learn about the trees in your area.

This fibrous lichen is often called beard lichen. It is sometimes incorrectly identified as a moss.

Looking at Lichens

Lichens grow almost everywhere in the world—even on the Arctic tundra and the Antarctic Peninsula. Lichens are actually two different types of plants growing together: algae cells growing amidst the weblike threads of a fungus. This living arrangement is called *symbiosis,* and both plants benefit from their intertwined lives. All lichens are symbionts. They can be found on rocks, tree bark, logs, and even gravestones.

Lichens can be very colorful, ranging from blue-green and sage-green to brown, yellow, orange, and red. Some look flat and leafy, others are crusty, and still others have branching stalks. Lichens are often good indicators of air quality, since they do not grow well if there is too much

sulfur-dioxide pollution. They have been used in medical research as antibiotics and have made good textile dyes. An avid birdwatcher may observe birds collecting lichens during the nesting season, since many species use lichens in building their nests. The rose robin of eastern Australia camouflages its nest with lichens and

The red caps on pale green stalks identify this lichen as a British soldier Cladonia. It is found in eastern North America.

so does the tiny ruby-throated hummingbird of North America.

Identification of lichens is difficult, because chemical tests and microscope study is usually necessary. But you don't need to identify an individual lichen to appreciate lichens' variety of colors, textures, and ability to grow in very harsh conditions. Lichens also make good subjects for outdoor photography. They give you a chance to experiment with shooting fine textures and subtle colors. If you want to photograph lichens, try shooting them after a rain or a heavy fog. They look their best when damp.

Try This!

Many lichen species grow flat on tree trunks or rocks and look a little like green lace doilies. They grow *very* slowly outward, creating a bigger and bigger "doily" or "medallion." You can easily find out just how fast (or slow) a lichen grows.

Many lichens grow like green "doilies" on the trunks of trees.

First, look for a small or medium lichen—one that is smaller than your palm.

Make a round spot on the tree bark, using a colored crayon or lumber marker, just above and below the lichen. These are your register marks.

Now place a clear sheet of acetate or plastic right over the lichen. A plastic bag cut open so that it lies flat will work fine.

Use a crayon, grease pencil, or marker to trace the register dots on your plastic. Continue to hold the plastic steadily in place, and now trace the outline of the lichen directly on the plastic.

Write the date and location on the plastic. Tie a ribbon or landscaper's tape around the tree to help you remember exactly where your sample lichen is.

In six months return to the same lichen, and put the plastic right over it. Match up the register dots at the top and bottom, and look at the outline of your lichen. Has it spread out and grown a little? Trace the outline of it again, and you'll have an exact record of how much it has grown. You can keep this experiment going for years.

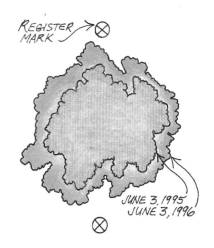

Tracing the outline of a lichen on clear plastic shows its outward growth from year to year.

chapter four

SOUNDS OF SUMMER

A Natural Background

Wherever you live, there are background noises so familiar that you ignore them. Indoors these sounds can include the whirr and click of computers, refrigerators, or heating systems. Outdoors you may hear traffic along a road or planes flying overhead.

Now try to become familiar with the *natural* background sounds in your neighborhood. Close your eyes for a minute and listen to any natural outdoor sounds around you, like the steady patter of rain or the breeze causing leaves to flutter. Then make a note of specific, individual sounds of birds or other wildlife. Here are a few examples.

the continuous buzzing of grasshoppers in a field

a young bird getting fed by its parents or the parents' excited calls

the first frog that starts a chorus of other frogs singing

Natural sounds change with the time of day and the seasons. Writing down the day-to-day

If this newly hatched killdeer chick is approached too closely, the parents' excited calls and dramatic wing-dragging acts will lead the offender away.

sounds of nature around you will help you become familiar with the activities of birds, frogs, insects, and other wildlife in your area.

Bird Songs

Birds make an amazing variety of sounds: whistling, wheezing, sharp screams, gentle twittering, crackling, and gurgling are just a few noises you'll hear. How could anyone remember them all? No one knows *all* the bird songs in

Like many songbirds, this yellow warbler sings from the top of an exposed twig. It is common throughout most of North America.

the world, but you can learn to identify some of the bird songs in your own neighborhood. It's just like meeting a new friend and getting used to that person's voice. Once you "meet" a few birds and get used to their songs, it will be easy to remember them.

You probably know some bird sounds already: the coo of a city pigeon, the quacking of ducks in a park, and the twittering of swallows on a telephone line. It won't be hard to learn a few new sounds.

The rapid, twittering calls of swallows and martins may be familiar in your neighborhood. This is a North American tree swallow.

Start Listening Right Now

When you hear a bird singing, try to locate where the sound is coming from. A bird may sing from a fence, a rooftop, the ground, or high in a tree. Move toward that sound to see if you can find the individual bird that is singing. You may need binoculars to see it clearly. Make a note of the general shape, color, and size of the bird. Noticing these details will help you describe the bird to a local birdwatcher or park ranger, who may be able to identify it. (See chapter 1, Wildlife Watching, to learn about field marks.)

Birds, like this male American robin, that live near houses and gardens frequently choose a post or fence to sing from.

Listen to a bird's song closely, and imagine how you could repeat, write, or describe it to someone else.

Here are some examples of written song descriptions.

 two short chirps and a burr: CHIP, CHIP, BRRRRR

 a flutelike song that spirals downward

a series of short notes that get faster and faster, like a small ball bouncing

When you hear a song, try writing down what you think the song sounded like. Some people think the American goldfinch has a song that sounds like "potato CHIP, potato CHIP, chip, chip."

Some bird songs are easy to remember. This ovenbird's call is a clear "teacher, teacher, teacher!"

Go out with a birdwatching group, and ask the leader to identify any songs the group hears.

Watch and listen to the most common birds around you: starlings, pigeons, or sparrows in the city.

When you hear a bird singing, try to get close enough to see its size, shape, color, or pattern. Make a note of its behavior and the surrounding habitat. These are the clues that will help a naturalist or experienced birdwatcher identify the bird for you.

Don't forget that many bird species sing in the early evening or at night. Around the world, most owls only call at night or on overcast, dark days. In North America, Great Britain, and Europe thrushes have *crepuscular* songs. That means they sing in the dusk or early evening.

Draw Your Own Sonogram!

You can draw a sort of picture of what you have heard to help you remember a song. A song with one long note and three higher short ones would look like this.

— — —

Write or draw anything that will help you remember the sounds.

Here are other ways to learn bird songs.

Listen to a recording or tape of bird songs. Be sure it presents species actually found in *your* area!

You can become familiar with many bird calls by listening to the most common birds in your area, such as geese, pigeons, or swallows. This is a gaggle of Canada geese.

Don't Be Fooled!

In the woods of North America, the high, frantic chattering of a red squirrel is often mistaken for the call of a bird. Don't assume you know the source of a noise. Always try to get a look at the noise-maker itself before you decide it's a bird.

Many birds are good mimics. You may hear a jay give the screaming call of a hawk or a North American mockingbird make a sound like a falcon.

You might find a small group of birds making excited or irritated "whisking" sounds or chipping sounds together. This may be an alarm signal. Look around for a cat or check the trees nearby for a hawk. The birds are using their alarm calls to make sure other birds know danger is nearby.

Many bird species around the world are excellent mimics. This is a mockingbird, common throughout much of North America.

Insect Sounds

During the warmer parts of the year, you can hear all types of insect sounds. Here are some insects you are likely to hear almost anywhere in the world.

Honeybees, Bumblebees, and Carpenter Bees

The larger bees make the largest sounds! It's easy to hear their low, sleepy drone as they visit one flower after another, sipping nectar and collecting pollen. Most large bees can be watched safely, as long as you stand still and don't interfere with their work.

The sleepy buzz of a bumblebee at work is a hallmark sound of high summer.

Crickets

These common insects are often seen in fields and gardens, but they also come into our homes as the weather gets cooler. The trilling or chirping song is made by the male as he scrapes one wing over the other. A raised pattern of ridges on the outer wings helps create the sound. Females can easily be identified by their thin long *ovipositor,* which is used to deposit eggs in the ground. It looks like a stinger, but it isn't.

This close-up of the wings of a male cricket shows the pattern of raised ridges that is rubbed to produce its song.

Generally, the warmer it is, the faster the male cricket will chirp. As the outdoor temperatures get colder, the song slows down.

Watch It Happen!

Catch a male cricket in a large jar and add some grasses, leaves, and a small piece of bread or fruit for food. Keep the cricket overnight in a quiet place and listen for his song. If you are patient and lucky, you can catch him in the act of singing, with his wings slightly raised.

Grasshoppers, Locusts, and Katydids

These insects make sounds by scraping their wings together, or by rubbing their hind legs against their outer wings. These buzzing, ripping sounds are called *stridulations.* Males usually stridulate the most, or they are much louder than females. Some grasshoppers can also make a snapping sound with their wings as they take flight. Some species are able to make more than one type of noise.

The "ears" of grasshoppers, locusts, and katydids are located in different places on different species. Some have an ear, called a *tympanum,* on each side of the abdomen. Others have a tympanum on each front leg.

Try This!

On North American katydids, you can see each tympanum as a curved, brown spot on the front legs. Catch a katydid in a field or meadow by "sweeping" back and forth with a field net. Then use a magnifying lens or loupe to see the tympanum closely. Katydids may be known as great green grasshoppers in Great Britain and as green-leaf grasshoppers in Australia. In North America, the true katydid of the eastern states is known for its call that sounds like "katy-did, katy-didn't."

Other Insect Noisemakers

Cicadas are among the loudest insects in the world. During hot, dry weather, these large insects grind out a nerve-wracking buzz that can be unforgettable. In Australia some species are called greengrocers, yellow Mondays, Mundys, or cherry-noses. Other species of cicadas around the world are called locusts or harvest-flies, but they are not related to true locusts or to flies. They belong to their own family, the Cicadidae. Some species of cicada spend as many as 17 years underground, as wingless nymphs, feeding on the sap from roots.

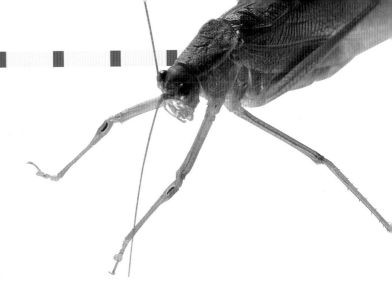

When the young nymphs mature, they dig out of the soil, climb up onto tree trunks and shrubs, and molt their skins. The winged adult cicadas then fly up into trees to sing their buzzing, droning songs, which are a hallmark of summer.

The larvae (or grubs) of beetles can be heard during the summer, too. Many species of wood-boring beetles around the world have larvae that can be heard as they chew through wood—indoors or outdoors! Some beetle larvae can actually cause damage to furniture and house lumber. The larvae of pine sawyer beetles live under the bark of newly felled pine trees in North America. You can stand several feet away

Look at the joint on this bush katydid's front legs for a curved, brown spot. That's the katydid's tympanum, or "ear," at each joint.

Bright leaf-green, this North American bush katydid is camouflaged well as it sings among grasses and weeds.

Here is the molted skin of a cicada nymph. This empty shell looks exactly like the nymph which has lived underground, feeding on the sap of roots.

from a fresh pine log and clearly hear these grubs grind and creak, as they chew away at the wood. These noisy larvae remain under the pine bark all winter, emerging as large beetles the following year. Adult pine sawyer beetles can be found on pine logs where they will later lay their eggs.

Frogs and Toads

Frogs and toads are amphibians. They need to spend some part of their lives in or near water, if only to mate and lay eggs. Many species of frog can be found on dry land, amidst ferns and mosses. Toads can be found in gardens, damp woods, and even the deserts of the American Southwest.

Frogs can sing while in water or on dry land. Some may climb onto water plants to sing.

Frogs and toads make sounds by releasing air from expandable air sacs under the chin or around the neck. These sounds can be heard as a croak, groaning, steady trill, or peep. Distance can distort the true sound of a toad or frog, so that some of their songs sound like the jingling of sleigh bells or like someone hammering on wood far away in a swamp. One North American

This American toad is a common amphibian that can be heard singing on warm nights. Its song is a steady trill.

species sounds like two stones being tapped or clicked together.

In general, the bigger the frog, the deeper its call. Tiny tree frogs have high peeps, while big bullfrogs have low croaks.

Patience and Stealth Needed

It can be very difficult to track down a frog or toad by its voice. You need to be very quiet and patient. As soon as you get close or make the slightest sound, the frog may stop singing or jump into the water. Plan ahead if you want to go out looking for amphibians at night. You'll need protection from mosquitoes, and you could get wet! Don't forget a flashlight, and give yourself plenty of time to stalk, wait, and watch.

Many frogs around the world have declined in their populations. If you catch a frog to study in a jar, take notes accurately on its size, color, and the habitat it was found in. Then let it go in the same area you found it.

Wetland Walks

Some nature centers and parks organize summer wetland walks in the evenings. Take advantage of these outings to learn about the amphibians in your area. Let the group leader know you are interested in identifying frog and toad calls.

You may also find recordings and tapes available of frog and toad calls, so you can learn about the different sounds on your own!

WATERWAYS & SEASHORES

Swamps, Bogs, and Ponds

There are many different types of water areas to investigate on your nature outings: natural ponds, bogs, red maple swamps, canebrakes, wet meadows, woodland streams, and farm ponds—just to name a few. These fresh-water habitats may be large or small, in open sun or in cool shade, and all are likely to be the home of fascinating animals and plants. Planning a hike in these areas can be a buggy, wet experience, however. Here are some hints for being comfortable.

- Bring along insect repellent. (See chapter 10, Country Comforts.)

- Wear long sleeves and long pants. Bring a jacket.

A woodland pool can attract a variety of wildlife and may be the habitat of many unusual wildflowers.

Plan your trip on a cool, breezy day.

Wear waterproof boots. Most large parks have boardwalks that span boggy areas, but you should be prepared for a wet trail.

Bring a pair of dry socks, especially for an all-day hike.

A sturdy hiking stick can help you get around wet places.

Wetland Wildflowers

Some of the world's most beautiful wildflowers can be found only in bogs and swamps. Orchids, sundews, pitcher plants, and arums thrive only in wet areas where there are plenty of biting insects. Finding these unusual plants makes a "bog slog" worth the effort.

Found only in boggy, wet habitats, this North American wild calla is a member of the Arum family. In Great Britain the lords-and-ladies wildflower is very similar; it is a member of the same family.

Fortunately, some parks and sanctuaries have labeled unique wetland wildflowers that can be viewed from raised wooden walks. Use the opportunity of finding these wonderful plants to write detailed field notes, take photographs, or create drawings. You may never return to these exact spots again, and you may never see the same species again. Take your time and record your observations carefully.

Small Wonders

Insects are among the most interesting animals to observe in wetland habitats. Watch for these common insects.

Watch dragonflies hunting for smaller insects; they catch them on the wing! Male dragonflies choose a lookout post, like the tip of a twig or leaf, to defend the area from other males. Watch for a dragonfly zooming off his perch to chase away another one.

Watch the surface of water for movement. You may see waterstriders "skating" across the surface or backswimmers "rowing" through the water. Look for diving beetles. Some swim underwater and can dive easily; others, called whirligigs, swirl in circles on the surface.

A dragonfly stops to rest just above the water. Note that the front pair of wings are a different shape than the hind wings!

Life on the Edge

The edge, bank, or perimeter of a pond or river is where animals come for water, take shelter, or rest. Berry plants and other food plants often grow in abundance. Stand quietly, and use your binoculars like a spy to scan along the edge of a pond, following the perimeter. Here are some things to look and listen for.

Look at floating objects along the edge, such as logs or lily pads. You may see not just frogs and dragonflies, but turtles sunning themselves and even a mother duck trailed by her ducklings.

Look for herons or egrets.

Look among the tall reeds and cattails in the spring. Small birds nesting at the water's edge may sit at the tops of tall reeds to sing or come out to observe your movements. If they seem to make a fuss as you move, you may be too close to a nest.

Scan the steep banks at the side of a river or stream. Holes in the exposed

Many types of songbirds nest near ponds and can be seen singing from the tops of plants near the water's edge. This is a North American red-winged blackbird.

dirt may be the nests of kingfishers, swallows, or small mammals.

Listen for the rattling call of a kingfisher as it flies across its territory.

Listen for the startled squawk or bleat of a frog, just before it leaps into the water for safety.

Many different species of heron, egret, and bittern can be found near ponds and rivers. This is a green heron from the United States.

Hiding among the grasses of a meadow is a North American leopard frog. Many species of frog can be found on dry land.

Keep an Eye on the Sky

The osprey, or fish eagle, lives in Great Britain, Europe, North America, and Australia. This large raptor hunts for fish in large ponds, lakes, and coastal areas, diving to catch fish with its sharp talons and then adjusting its prey headfirst to carry it more easily. Ospreys circle and hover above the water as they look for fish.

Also look up to find kingfishers hovering in place as they hunt for fish. You can also find swallows almost anywhere in the world, crisscrossing over the water as they snap up small insects on the wing. Look in overhanging branches for roosting herons, egrets, and kingfishers.

Ospreys feed on fish and are sometimes called fish eagles. They are found on every continent except Antarctica.

Look Down at This!

The bull-head lily of North America is a common species of water lily in small ponds and lakes. The yellow water lily of Great Britain is very closely related.

Tracks of mammals and water birds can often be found in mud or sand at the edge of the water. You may be able to tell if they came to the water only to drink and then moved away or if they stayed to rest or eat.

Look down into the water of ponds or lakes for the *nests* of fish! Sunfish, such as bluegills and pumpkinseeds in North America, make shallow, rounded nests near the shore and usually stay nearby to defend their territory. You can lie on the bank or on a pier to watch these fish at work.

Get a close look at life at the bottom of a pond or stream. Use an old plastic container to scoop out some muck and water from the bottom, and pour it into a flat container (an old cake pan is fine). Let the mud and debris settle. Soon you'll see a variety of small insects: the larvae of flies, beetles, mosquitoes, and dragonflies. Tiny crustaceans, leeches, and planarians may be in the water, too. Use a loupe or magnifying glass to study these tiny creatures; then return them to their habitat. One panful of tiny pond animals should give you the opportunity to observe their *adaptations* for swimming, camouflage, hiding, and catching and eating food.

Be sure to wash your hands thoroughly afterward because some microorganisms in pond or stream water could make you sick.

Beachside Botany: The Shore and Coast

Most plants you see near the coast or at the beach are uniquely adapted to a salt-air, seaside habitat. Whenever you are near the shore, look for plants with thickened stems and leaves. These help the plants withstand the salt spray and driving winds. Leaves of some plants may feel leathery or waxy. Look at the trees along the shore, and you may see that they are stunted or twisted from winds.

Not Just Dune Grass

Along sandy dunes and banks near the coast, you will probably find clumps of grasses with thin, stiff leaves. On coastlines around the world

The piping plover is a rare species of shorebird in North America; it is protected by United States and Canadian law. It nests and feeds along the shore and coast.

these tough *dune grasses* and other seaside plants camouflage the nests of shorebirds. Many of these birds are rare or threatened with extinction. Avoid walking through any dune grass areas so that you don't accidentally trample a nest or disturb mother birds incubating eggs. Prevent pets from roaming where shorebirds may be nesting; many nests and chicks of rare birds are destroyed each year by cats and dogs.

Walking the Line

At the beach walk along the *sea wrack;* that's the messy tangle of seaweed and debris left by the waves of the last highest tide. This is where you'll find many specimens of plants and animals from the ocean that you'd never be able to see otherwise. The best time to investigate the sea wrack is after a storm or full moon. Look for the egg cases of skates (they're called mermaid's purses), the remains of sea urchins, strings of whelk eggs, and shells with barnacles attached. Broken fragments of shells may not look beautiful at first glance, but they show the interior design and structure of a shell and make excellent subjects for photography and field drawings.

You'll probably find several species of seaweed. Seaweed is classified as marine algae and may be dark green, bright light green, reddish, or brown. It is anchored to underwater rocks by *holdfasts.* After a storm, seaweed is often torn up and washed ashore; then you'll have an opportunity to look at the holdfasts closely. Some are like tiny disks, while others have small fingerlike projections. The puffed-out blisters or bladders on some species help keep the plant buoyant in the ocean. You can take samples of seaweed and make a permanent study collection. (See chapter 11, Saving It.)

Be Careful!

You may have to climb about on rocks near the ocean to look into tide pools. This is where you'll see shrimp and other small crustaceans. These are what shorebirds eat. You might also find small crabs and colorful anemones attached to rocks. But be very careful, and watch out for slippery, seaweed-covered rocks.

Another hazard is venomous sea creatures. Live cone shells in tropical areas can sting, and the spines of some living sea urchins are poisonous. Even some of the smallest jellyfish can be dangerous. Always remember: you never have to touch or handle any wild creature, ever!

Hunting for fish and frogs at the water's edge, this great blue heron is the largest heron in North America. Observers in Great Britain, Europe, and Australia are likely to see other species of heron near ponds and rivers.

The black-bellied plover is frequently seen during migration in North America. In Great Britain this species is called the gray plover. It feeds on tiny crustaceans along the shoreline.

Watching Water Birds

Birds that hunt for their food by wading along the edges of ponds and rivers or in the shallow water at the coast are often called *wading birds.* Around the world, some of the largest wading birds include herons and egrets. Whether you live in Australia, Europe, Great Britain, or North America, you are likely to see these long-legged, sword-billed birds. Open wet fields attract cattle egrets, a smaller species found nearly worldwide. Take the time to observe how herons and egrets hunt and feed. They usually proceed slow-

A long, thin downward-curved bill helps identify this glossy ibis. Becoming more common on the Atlantic coast of the United States, this same species is also found in eastern Australia!

ly and patiently, carefully stalking their prey in shallow water, and then jab with lightning speed at a frog or fish! In Australia, birdwatchers may see spoonbills, storks, and ibis; all these birds have different feeding habits.

Look at Those Legs

Watching wading birds provides a good opportunity to see the difference in the ages of birds. The color of the legs of many species changes as they get older. In North America, the snowy egret has greenish legs within its first year of life. But by the time it's about one year old, its legs have become black, with bright yellow feet.

Found in most of the United States, this snowy egret hunts for fish in a coastal marsh. The large egret of Australia is a closely related species.

The Shorebird Migration

To ornithologists *shorebirds* are a distinct group of birds that includes many different families: plovers, sandpipers, gulls, and avocets, for example. Small shorebirds are collectively called "peeps" by birdwatchers, because of the sound they make.

During the autumn in North America, flocks of shorebirds head south. After flying great distances, these birds need a safe place to rest and eat. Unfortunately, people and dogs running

The sanderling is a shorebird often seen in large flocks during migration. This species is found in North America, Great Britain, Europe, and along the coasts of Australia.

along the beach frighten away flocks of exhausted shorebirds. If you are out birdwatching where migrating shorebirds have come to feed and rest, do not disturb them. Don't let children or pets run out onto the sand and force the birds to fly away. The next beach may not be safe!

Watch these interesting birds from a distance, using binoculars. Observe their feeding habits, and watch how they rest. Most sleep standing on one leg, and most can be observed preening vig-

orously. Look for these details: beak color, shape, and length. Some have long beaks that curve up or down slightly, and some have thick beaks, others thin. Look at the color and length of the legs, and note any contrasting color of the tail and the rump area, when the birds fly. Watch a flock fly together. They are almost like a school of fish, turning and veering and rising together as a group!

Go on a Whale-Watch Cruise!

In many coastal communities, whale-watch cruise boats have become a popular attraction to tourists and naturalists. Depending on where you live, a whale-watch trip may last just a couple of hours, or it may involve most of the day! The cruise should give you the opportunity to observe other marine mammals also, such as dolphins and seals. In addition, you may see *oceanic birds*, such as puffins, gannets, petrels, phalaropes, and shearwaters.

Before you go, call the cruise office first. Get details on departure times, sea conditions, and the expected sightings. You may have to make reservations. Here are some hints for having a successful whale-watch trip.

Listen to a marine weather report, and choose a day with calm seas.

Bring sunglasses and a brimmed hat. You will be gazing out over the ocean, with the bright sun glaring on it.

It may not be a warm adventure. Expect a cold, driving wind, and a wet spray. Take along a sweater and a jacket.

Bring binoculars. Whales and seabirds may be far from the boat.

Just before it dives, the back and dorsal fin of this humpback whale are easy to see. The small bump at the far right is the whale's spout hole (blowhole) on the top of its head.

The flukes (tail) of a humpback whale, as it dives to feed. Scratches and scars are often seen on a whale's flukes. The white areas are typical markings on older humpbacks.

As your whale-watch boat leaves the harbor, you may see gulls, terns, pelicans, and other birds. Bring your binoculars!

Ask the crew what to look for. Many boats have a staff naturalist and posters or leaflets about the whales and seabirds you can expect to see.

If you're worried about getting seasick, plan on having a light breakfast that morning. Avoid fatty, greasy, or strongly flavored food the night before the trip and on the morning of the trip. Bring along hard candies and light snacks such as crackers, biscuits, or granola bars. Also, many people feel that ginger helps prevent motion sickness and calms stomach upset. Ginger tea, ginger cookies, or a small chunk of crystallized ginger may help.

Don't stand near anyone smoking a cigarette or pipe, and avoid diesel fumes; strong odors may make you feel sick. Stay in the fresh air. Don't decide to stick it out in a confined, stuffy, small cabin.

If you normally use medication for motion sickness, remember to take it as prescribed, usually well *before* the trip begins. Try wearing wristbands designed to prevent motion sickness, available at some pharmacies.

Concentrate on studying the unique ocean animals that you may never have the opportunity to see again! Focus on the behavior and flight abilities of the seabirds.

Be on the Alert!

A whale-watch cruise is not like a show at a commercial marine aquarium. Strict laws prevent cruise boats from approaching too closely to the whales so that family groups are not disturbed. Whale sightings may be quick and fleeting. You'll need to be alert so that you don't miss a thing!

Carry binoculars since whales and dolphins may be some distance away. You may only catch a few seconds' glimpse of a whale's fluke (its tail) or a momentary view of a whale's dorsal fin and back, before it dives. If you're lucky, you'll see and *hear* a whale spouting, as it blows out a great gush of air. On some boats, observers are asked to shout "Thar she blows!" and point out where the spout was seen, so that others can see it, too.

WINTER WONDERS

The winter months are cold and snowy in many parts of North America, Great Britain, and northern Europe.

Observing Mammals

The winter months are harsh and difficult for wildlife in many parts of North America, Great Britain, and Europe. Temperatures in the United States and Canada often plunge below zero.

In the coldest areas of North America, mammals like bears, marmots, woodchucks, skunks, and chipmunks hibernate during the winter. They spend the entire cold season in underground dens. Many mammals, however, are active throughout the winter: red squirrels, gray squirrels, flying squirrels, mice, and voles. But even these hardy animals spend stormy days or very cold days in a den, nest, or hollow tree.

Here are some of the best places and times to observe mammals in winter.

When a snowstorm has passed and calm, sunny weather returns.

At a winter feeding station set up for birds. Squirrels and mice visit these sites for seeds and corn.

After a spell of bitter cold temperatures.

In a dense grove of evergreen shrubs or trees. These provide protection from wind, and a safe place to rest.

Gray squirrels are active throughout the winter in Canada and the northern United States. During severe weather, they may stay in their dens for a few days.

Small holes in the snow where mice or weasels have burrowed in or come up from under a layer of snow. As the winter passes and the surface snow melts away, look in the same area to find a maze of exposed tunnels.

Near a stand of shrubs which have abundant berries or seeds.

Detective Work

You may not actually *see* any mammals on an outdoor hike, but you might find evidence of their presence instead. Here are a few examples.

An old bird's nest has been taken over by a mouse or squirrel. It will add leaves and grasses to make a snug winter hideaway.

Tracks in the snow may lead to a hiding place in a dense brush pile or wood pile. This is the type of shelter that a rabbit or hare would use.

A small pile of light brown, rounded droppings (feces, or *scat*) is a telltale clue that a rabbit or hare lives and feeds nearby. Smaller, darker droppings from squirrels and mice can be found near feeding stations for birds.

The winter den of a snowshoe hare; ice crystals surround the entrance.

The Right Track

Animal tracks in *deep* snow are difficult to see clearly. Here are a few hints for finding good, clear tracks.

Try making observations after the first light snowfall of the season. Tracks made in a thin layer of new snow are very clear.

Go out while the snow is new and fresh. Snow "ages" after several hours and even more after a few days. It becomes compact and hard, and the feet and toes of animals don't leave a perfect impression.

Look for sheltered areas where the snow lies flat and even. Wind can ruin the outline and details of a track; fine particles of snow are blown away from the edges.

Tracks of a North American gray squirrel, found in a thin layer of snow.

Try It Yourself

Make some tracks in new snow with your boots, your gloved hands, or a sled. Look at these impressions closely, and make a note of how

The tracks of an American crow, walking over new snow. The hind claw has left a "drag line" in the snow as the crow walks.

clear and sharp these fresh tracks look. The next day look at them again. You'll probably notice some changes. "Old" tracks often look larger than new tracks. That's because the snow has settled a little or melted back. The outer edges may have crumbled away due to wind during the night. Details on animal tracks, such as claw marks, would be missing.

When you do find animal tracks, note their pattern, shape, and whether there are claw marks. The tracks of domestic cats are small and rounded, and they don't usually show claw marks. But the tracks of dogs and foxes almost always show the impression of toenails.

As Clean As Snow?

A blanket of fresh, new snow isn't always perfectly clean and white! Look closely for these details.

Snowfleas are tiny insects (*not* fleas at all) that can be found in vast numbers on the surface of the snow.

Birch seeds may be scattered on the surface of the snow as birds feed on them in the trees above. They look like tiny "eagles" or a fleur-de-lis design.

Look at individual particles of snow as they fall on your jacket. You may find six-sided snowflakes, pelletlike graupel, or needlelike crystals. Use a magnifying glass for a better look. Compare these shapes with frost on a window or car windshield.

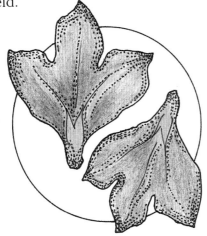

Birch seeds can be found on the snow as birds take apart the seed clusters or as winter winds blow them down. (Seeds are shown enlarged.)

Construction Sites

On your winter walks, you may easily find evidence of homes made and used during the summer by a variety of wildlife.

Bird Nests After the trees lose their leaves, it's easy to see where birds have nested. Noting these nesting sites will help you to learn where to look for birds during the summer!

Cocoons You may find fuzzy or papery cocoons of moths on twigs, branches, or tall grasses. The moth pupa inside will be protected during the winter months; a fully developed moth will emerge from the cocoon when the temperature and sunlight provide the perfect signals of spring. *Don't* bring a cocoon indoors, or the moth will emerge in your house and have no chance of survival.

Try this "knock, knock, who's there?" experiment: Tap gently on the side of a hollow snag or old birdhouse with a stick. You might see a sleepy mouse or squirrel poke its head out the hole to see what the noise is about! Small mammals often use a hollow trunk or old bird's nest as a snug winter shelter.

DON'T do this during the summer when birds may be in the nest, incubating eggs.

Clay or Mud Nests of Wasps Many wasp species around the world construct clay nests for their young. During the winter some of these may be abandoned and empty, but others may *not* be. Don't bring these fragile nests indoors!

Hornet Nests These large paper nests can be

the size of a basketball! If the temperatures are below freezing, it's safe to look at one closely, but NEVER bring a nest like this indoors!

Winter Birds

In cold climates, most birds that eat insects have to migrate. They fly to areas that are warmer, where there are plenty of flying insects. In many parts of North America, Great Britain, or Europe you can expect most insect-eating birds to fly south in the autumn. Seed-eating birds, however, may stay in your area year-round. Seed-eaters include many different finch and sparrow species.

Owls can hunt mice and voles all winter long. This is a North American great horned owl.

Seed-eating birds, like this white-throated sparrow, can be seen throughout most of the winter in North America.

Birds that stay throughout the year are often called "resident" species. Resident birds in North America, Great Britain, and Europe may include owls, woodpeckers, creepers, nuthatches, and chickadees. The British relatives of chickadees are known as marsh tits and willow tits. Many smaller birds can continue to eat insect material during the winter, because they peck away at bark, finding insect eggs, pupae, or grubs in rotting logs and stumps. Crows, ravens, jays, and magpies stay year-round in most areas because they are scavengers, feeding on carrion (such as road-killed animals). They also feed on grain, seeds, and suet at winter feeding stations.

During a severe winter, some birds need to fly beyond their normal winter range to find food. This snowy owl has migrated south from Canada to spend the winter on the coast of Maine.

In Australia and New Zealand, most land birds don't need to migrate to a warmer climate. But some species, like the Bourke's parrot and budgerigars (parakeets), are nomadic. They roam from one area to another, sometimes in large groups, looking for the best food and water. The sacred kingfisher may also migrate, leaving the coastal areas to spend the winters inland.

Starting a Feeding Station

This cardinal is feeding on sunflower seeds that have been scattered on the ground.

Hanging feeders filled with sunflower seed or thistle seed will attract goldfinches and other seed-eaters in North America.

Birdwatchers around the world feed wild birds so that they can get a closer look at the variety of species in their neighborhood. Here are some ways you can start a simple feeding station.

Scatter seed right on the ground. Find a flat area that has evergreen shrubs or trees or a dense hedge nearby. Birds prefer to feed where there is good *cover,* such as bushes or a hedgerow, where they can hide or rest after eating. Seed scattered on the ground will attract doves, quail, sparrows, and finches.

Use a platform feeder. This is a flat tray raised off the ground. Spread seed on the top of an old barrel or bench; a large, flat tree stump; or a flat piece of wood nailed to a post.

Try a hanging feeder. Many styles and shapes of commercial feeders are available. If the feeder is hung where squirrels can climb onto it, they may chew it to bits and shreds in just a few days!

Be Patient

Don't get discouraged if no birds show up at your feeder right away. It can take weeks or even months for a feeding station to become successful. You might try using different seeds or a variety of seeds. Remember to start feeding in the autumn. Don't wait until the middle of winter!

For the safety of the birds, keep all dogs and cats AWAY from your feeder. Don't place a feeder too close to a window. Birds that are suddenly frightened by a cat or a person will fly off in a panic. They may strike a window with full force and be killed.

Once your feeding station becomes active, you should rake away old seed hulls. Combine them with grass and leaves as mulch and use them as compost in your garden.

A black-capped chickadee hovers momentarily as it decides whether to land on the author's glove for seeds.

A safe landing! This North American chickadee seems to have second thoughts about getting a handout. The willow tits and marsh tits of Great Britain and Europe are closely related and similar in appearance.

Trees in Winter

Even if you are knee-deep in snow, there are green plants to observe in winter. Evergreens are trees or shrubs that have green leaves throughout the winter season. Some examples of evergreen trees in northern climates are spruce, fir, pine, hemlock, yew, and juniper.

All of these trees do lose their old leaves, and new ones grow out—but they never lose all their leaves at one time. Take a close look at the leaves of an evergreen with a magnifying lens or loupe. The underside of each leaf may look entirely different than the upper surface.

Even the trees that have lost their leaves for the winter can be interesting to study during the cold season. Here are some observations you can make on the trees in your own neighborhood.

Look at the bark for evidence of animal activity. There may be claw marks from climbing animals, such as squirrels.

Holes in the bark may have been made by woodpeckers or other birds searching for insects.

Wood-boring beetles may have damaged the bark.

You may find the eggs of insects on the underside of leaves and branches. These will overwinter and hatch in the spring.

Find out which trees in your area have berries or large seeds that birds and other animals eat. Some berries may be ignored until the middle of winter, after freezing temperatures have softened or aged the fruit.

Look for lichens, fungi, or moss growing on the tree trunk.

Find a section where the bark has grown over to protect an injury, such as that from a nail, lightning strike, or storm damage.

Look for buds on each small branch or twig. Many people think that buds are formed during the spring, but they've been there all winter! Use a magnifying lens or loupe to see the details such as fine hairs and the individual scales that make up each bud.

Throughout the winter, pine trees retain their green, needlelike leaves.

A North American downy woodpecker hunts for insects eggs and pupae on the trunk of a maple. Note the short, curved talons which help the bird keep a grip on the tree bark.

Shrubs with berries attract birds all winter. This is a North American staghorn sumac.

No Snow at All?

In some places the winter season doesn't get snowy or cold at all. You may have a few cool, wet months instead. Steady rain or cold, damp days can certainly seem boring. But there's still a lot you can do!

Visit a nature center or museum that has special exhibits for the rainy season.

Listen to audiotapes of bird songs or frogs so that you can be ready to identify common species when the weather is better.

Use your local library to find out what native animal species depend on a soaking rainfall to survive. Large animals will need pools for drinking water. Amphibians need wet swamps and pools long enough for their eggs to hatch and their young to mature.

Learn about the plants in your area that need a cold or wet season to survive. Some wildflower seeds must have an extended cold season or else they won't germinate. Some tree species bloom profusely only after a heavy rain.

Make plans to visit several different habitats as soon as the wet season ends. You're likely to see plants and flowers that you won't find the rest of the year!

chapter seven

BACKYARD SANCTUARY

Water Works

Almost anyone can attract birds, mammals, colorful insects, and other wildlife to their own yard by providing water, food, or shelter.

Supplying water is one of the easiest ways to bring wildlife closer to your home. If you don't have a pond or stream nearby, you can simply set out a birdbath, or just a flat pan of water on the ground. Most wildlife photographers, artists, and birdwatchers provide water for birds and other animals, so that they can have year-round opportunities at good shots and close-up viewing.

Here are a few tips for success.

Keep the bath or water pan clean and filled—about 1½ inches (about 4 cm) deep.

Always set the water in the same place.

Add some pebbles or a small rock in the pan. Birds seem more confident about stepping in.

During the winter, try putting warm water in a plastic pan. When the water freezes, you can just knock the ice out.

Some people use water heaters designed specifically for outdoor birdbaths.

Try hanging a drip bucket above the bath or pan. Make a pinhole in the bottom of a clean plastic container, so the water only drips out one drop at a time. Hang it above the pan to create a ripple effect. It should take several hours for the container to become empty.

Setting out a pan of fresh water is the easiest way to bring wildlife closer to your home.

In desert areas, a pan of water in a shaded area will even attract lizards! Try creating additional shade with some flat rocks or pieces of wood, propped up at one end with stones.

Shrubs, evergreen hedges, or a brush pile nearby provide safe roosting and hiding places for birds to rest and preen their feathers.

Don't forget to observe the smallest natural water sites: puddles. Butterflies frequently sip water from the edge of a puddle. Female potter wasps and other mud-using wasps come to a puddle to gather mud or clay. And several species of swallows and other birds around the world use mud to build their nests.

Flowers Are Food

Most flowers produce pollen and nectar. Some species, however, produce much more than others. Flowers can attract hummingbirds in North America, and they attract pollinating bees, wasps, butterflies, and beetles, no matter where you live!

You may need to visit a local gardening center or agricultural supplier to find out the best flowering plants and shrubs to use in your neighborhood. You can easily start out with plants in the mint family, since they are easy to start from seed or cuttings. Many types of mints produce abundant nectar and pollen. Here are some examples.

 peppermint and spearmint

 anise hyssop (*Agastache*)

 red tree-balm (*Monarda*)

A *flower and herb garden provides pollen and nectar to a variety of insects.*

 motherwort (*Leonurus*)

 red salvia

In addition to mints, these plants—thistles, honeysuckles, penstemons, cleomes, and jasmine—are also good.

Don't forget to visit your garden at dusk or at night to observe the moths that come to the flowers.

⫿⫿⫿⫿⫿⫿ *This red bee balm, a member of the mint family, will attract many types of butterflies and hummingbirds in North America.*

⫿⫿⫿⫿⫿⫿ *All types of thistles attract butterflies, moths, beetles, and bees.*

kitchen leftovers. Birds and small mammals often visit compost piles to scavenge.

Salt blocks or salt licks aren't actually food, but they provide salt and other minerals for deer, porcupine, and rabbits. In some areas, salt blocks are so successful, they are illegal to use during the hunting season.

Paint the trunk of a tree with "bug juice." Almost any mixture of honey, fruit juice, and molasses spread on tree bark will attract moths, butterflies, or beetles.

Spray an even mix of honey and water on garden leaves or ferns, using a plant mister or spray bottle. This will attract pollinating insects such as honeybees and bumblebees.

Let weeds grow up in one area as a border. Weed seeds are eaten by many bird species, and the flowers will be visited by a variety of insects.

Try This!

Here are some other ways to attract wildlife to your yard with food.

Plant shrubs, hedges, or vines that produce berries or seeds abundantly. Ask for advice from a garden center.

Try fastening half an orange to a branch or post. This often attracts birds that like fruits and berries.

Keep an eye on your garden compost heap, especially if you throw out

⫿⫿⫿⫿⫿⫿ *An overgrown border of weeds will attract pollinating insects, and birds will eat the weed seeds in the fall and winter.*

You can creatively use flowers, food plants, and water to bring wildlife quite close to your home. In many cases, you will be able to make observations right from your kitchen or bedroom windows.

This day-flying sphinx moth is a colorful visitor to a North American flower garden. Many people mistake these insects for hummingbirds. Sphinx moths, often called hawk moths, are found in North and South America, Europe, Great Britain, and Australia.

A Note of Caution

Do NOT leave meat, dog food, or cat food outdoors. These foods attract rats almost anywhere in the world. In North America, raccoons and skunks can become regular customers when pet food is left outside. Both of these mammals can carry rabies, distemper, or other diseases.

Building a Brush Pile

Naturalists and woodlot owners often build brush piles to provide shelter for wildlife. Loosely piled mounds of brush can be built at any time of year. They will be welcomed by small mammals and birds as safe hideouts. The topmost branches can become lookout points that are often chosen as a site for birds to sing from. Here's how to make a good brush pile.

Start out with large branches and sticks. You may need to push a branch or two firmly into the ground to support the others.

Add small sticks but leave plenty of open space.

Add prickly brambles or vines to discourage cats.

Top it off with a roof of evergreen branches or dry leaves.

Your finished brush pile should be about knee-high to waist-high.

Try building several brush piles. Each one will attract different animals, depending on where it is or how it is made. All brush piles settle, change shape, and decay, so you'll be able to start a new one from time to time!

Wildlife photographer Kevin Byron finishes a brush pile by adding a roof of pine boughs.

Nesting Boxes for Birds

Setting up a birdhouse or bird box is an excellent way to bring birds closer to your house. The type of house or box you should use in your area depends on the species found in your neighborhood. Most garden centers and feed or grain stores sell birdhouses. You can also buy kits containing precut wood pieces to assemble yourself. To build a bird-

Hanging up a birdhouse in the early spring is an excellent way to bring birds closer to your home.

An open garden shed can become the perfect nesting site for swallows and phoebes in North America.

house, you'll need to know specific measurements and entrance-hole diameters. That's because different bird species prefer to use different size boxes. You'll need to look at plans or to visit a nature center or garden store that specializes in bird-feeding and birdwatching sup-

plies. In North America, for example, a wren house should be only 4 inches (10 cm) wide on each side, 7 inches (17.5 cm) deep, with an entrance hole 1¼ (about 3.2 cm) inches in diameter. But for a bluebird, you need a box 5 inches (12.5 cm) wide on each side, about 11 inches (27.5 cm) deep, with an entrance hole 1½ inches (3.75 cm) in diameter.

Some whimsical commercial birdhouses have large entrance holes with a perch or peg. Unfortunately, those large entrances and pegs help less desirable species, such as house sparrows and starlings, get inside easily.

If you already have a nesting box hanging up that has not attracted any birds, try these ideas.

Take the box down and hang it in a different location.

Clean it out! There may have been mice nesting inside, or it may be filled with old nesting material.

Hang the box so that the entrance hole faces the opposite direction.

Birdhouses made by humans are not always successful. Birds often nest where you don't expect them to: under an eave, on a curving drainpipe, in an open garage or carport, and even on top of an outdoor security lamp that's lit all night!

Butterfly Roosts, Bat Houses, and Bee Boxes

Don't stop with a birdhouse. You can also put up artificial nesting sites for other wildlife as well. Here are some examples.

A *butterfly roosting box* is available in many

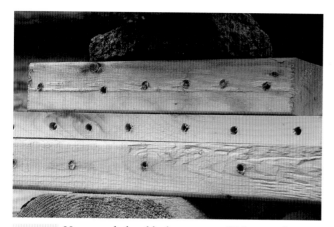

Homemade bee blocks attract wild bees and aphid-hunting wasps. Note that a few entrances are already sealed off with clay or resin.

garden stores and catalogs. This is a narrow wooden box with vertical slits in the front. Butterflies enter the slits to roost in the box during cold periods to *hibernate*. In very hot conditions, they crawl inside to *estivate*, escape the drying heat. These boxes are not always successful and may attract unwelcome spiders and insects, such as paper wasps.

Bat houses have become popular in North America in recent years. Available in garden centers and catalogs, instructions are included for hanging. Bats are terrific insect-control animals.

Bee boxes or *bee blocks* have been familiar to European gardeners for many years, but they have only just become popular in North America. These are untreated, unpainted wooden planks or blocks with holes drilled into them. Small wild bees and wasps use the holes to start nurseries for their young. Bees stock their nurseries with pollen. Female wasps fill the holes with garden pests for their larvae to feed on. Depending on the species, the wasps carry in cutworms and destructive caterpillars, aphids, or leafhoppers. When their nurseries are completed and stocked, the bees and wasps seal off the entrance hole with mud or clay. Some species use pitch or tree resins. Others camouflage the entrance with bits of grasses and plants.

These female wasps and bees are capable of stinging, just like other wasps and bees. However, they are usually only interested in their nesting duties, and they are normally peaceful and not aggressive. Unlike honeybees, they do not nest in huge hives.

Did You Know . . . ?

Across North America, domesticated honeybees have suffered a sharp decline. Huge numbers have been killed or weakened by disease and weather problems. Gardeners and farmers who depend on these insects to pollinate their crops are now encouraging wild native bees to nest near their gardens.

Backyard Surprises

Whether you have an extensive flower garden or a few pots of flowers on a balcony, you're likely to see wildlife—perhaps tiny beetles clambering about on your petunia or a perfectly camouflaged spider in the center of a daisy. You're also very likely to make many discoveries by accident. You might pick up an old broken clay flowerpot and find a toad or salamander underneath it. Or, as you pull aside a rotting board lying on the ground, a pair of bright emerald-green ground beetles scuttle away. Inside a shed or barn, you reach up for a rake or hoe you used

Working in a garden provides an excellent opportunity to observe insects and small mammals and to listen to birds.

Colorful caterpillars and other insects are frequently discovered by accident, while working outdoors. This is the larva of a North American cecropia moth.

just the other day, and you discover that a bird has started to build a nest on it.

Always keep alert for the tiniest clues to wildlife activity in your garden or around your house or apartment building. Every crevice in a cement foundation may shelter a beetle. The space under a loose shingle might be the winter home of a colorful moth. Each rotting board on the ground could be the home territory of a snake or salamander. You never know when or where you will have a surprise encounter with the natural world.

This graceful but fragile red eft was found under a board in the author's garden.

A garden is a veritable jungle that's full of surprises! Don't let yourself be distracted during your observations.

This American luna moth is a startling and beautiful specimen to any gardener and wildlife-watcher. Many different types of "moon moths" are found around the world.

Don't Get Distracted

Many people who spend time outdoors never hear or see the wildlife or wildflowers around them. Some work outdoors listening to a radio; others allow themselves to be interrupted by calls from a personal beeper. Even while walking down a park trail, hikers might fail to see a colony of rare orchids because their dog suddenly tugged on the leash. Radio music or the activity of a pet may distract you during the fleet-

Spider-watching takes time and patience. This American argiope, sometimes called the golden garden spider, creates a large geometric web.

ing moment it takes for a migrating peregrine falcon to zip by you.

All types of wildlife—birds, mammals, butterflies, digger wasps—move quickly about their daily activities. You will need to be alert so that you don't miss a thing! Even while standing and admiring your garden, you should try to remain focused and free of interruptions.

Some outdoor observations require time and patience, such as watching an orb-web spider weave its elaborate geometric web. If you plan to be outdoors to make wildlife observations, try to limit any distractions. That way, you don't miss out on any exciting events.

A Bird's-Eye View

Making a map of your home yard will help you learn where—and why—your best observations can be made. You just need to draw a rough picture of where your brush piles, birdhouses, or bee boxes are located, and you'll be able to get an overall view of how wildlife uses your yard. Try drawing in a mark or symbol each time you observe a particular bird or mammal. After several weeks, you'll have a good idea of its territory. Here are examples of things you may learn from your map.

You'll notice that your bee boxes could be shifted to a sunnier location at the opposite end of the garden.

The birdbath is far from the house and could be moved closer. That way, you'll be able to watch birds more closely.

The biggest brush pile is the one where you always see the rabbit. Maybe you could try to build another one.

Deer always seem to use the same trail, avoiding a neighboring lot where there are dogs. You'll know where to place a salt lick.

A wren house could be hung closer to your home (before the nesting season starts) so that you can watch new residents more easily.

Draw in a particularly interesting colony of wildflowers. The following summer, you'll be able to compare how the colony is doing. Will the colony expand or decline?

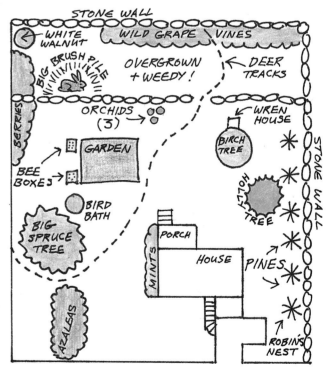

Drawing a simple map of your yard can help you decide where to place birdhouses, bee boxes, flowering plants, or brush piles.

the NATURALIST'S NOTEBOOK

Making Memories

Most people often write lists and reminders for themselves: shopping lists; schedules for meetings, classes, or sports events; or notes about phone calls to be made. We also keep a record of things we've already done, so that we have a more vivid memory of that event. That's why we take photos of family gatherings or keep used movie tickets. Reminders and written notes can also help us recall the details of outdoor experiences. Here are a few examples.

Gardeners put stakes and labels near their plants to identify seed rows or young seedlings.

Weather-watchers keep a daily log of temperatures, wind, and barometric readings.

Travelers and vacationers keep a journal of their tours.

We just *can't* remember all the details of day-to-day events, so we write them down.

Gardeners use stakes and labels to identify plants in their gardens and flowers started from seed. These are Australian Swan River daisies.

Field Notes

You may have already decided to keep a journal of your field notes. Field notes are written observations made while outdoors or at home, right after an outdoor hike. Here's how a daily nature notebook can help you.

It will accurately document your outdoor experiences.

You will be able to compare written notes from year to year to see if there are any changes in wildlife in your area.

Your observations will reveal the parts of your property that are most attractive to wildlife.

Your nature notebook will become a good record of exactly when and where you found local wildflowers. These are bunchberry flowers, sometimes called dwarf cornel.

Accurate notes will help you remember when unusual flowers are in bloom so that you don't miss out on seeing them! These orchids are called moccasin flowers or pink lady's slippers.

You'll have an accurate record of when and where you've had the best sightings. That way, you can return to exactly the same place!

Animals and plants common today may become rare within your lifetime. But your notes and drawings will provide a clear record of your observation of them.

Reptiles like this box turtle may be a rare encounter. It could be many years before you find one again!

Getting Started

Writing notes on a large wall calendar is a good way to start keeping a daily record of outdoor observations.

There are several different ways to start keeping notes about the wildlife or wildflowers that you observe.

Find a large wall calendar with big squares to write in. Just jot down your daily sightings of birds, insects, weather, or flowering plants. The biggest benefit is that you can look at the entire month at once to see how your observations change as the weather changes.

Use a datebook or an appointment book. Since there are several lines available for each day, you can write a more complete description of what you've seen. Be sure to get a datebook that lies flat when it's open so that it's easy to write in.

You may want to keep a nature notebook for recording your observations in just one habitat. A raised boardwalk over this bog provides a view of plants and birds that may only be seen in this unique habitat.

Write in a notebook. Don't use a notebook that's too small. You'll feel as though you have to limit your writing to one small page a day. Small notebooks are usually difficult to write in. You may even want to start a notebook that just focuses on one animal or one area, like your garden or an old cow field. You could keep a specialized notebook of bird observations or have a notebook only for insects.

Pens and Pencils

Here are some writing tips.

Use a pen with black ink. Colored ink sometimes fades after a few years.

If you want to use a pencil, try a mechanical pencil, sometimes called a drafting pencil or architect's pencil. The leads inside are always sharp.

Left-handers may want to try using wire-bound notebooks so that the notebook can be folded back and the spine is not in the way. Notebooks designed for shorthand or stenography have the binding at the top, and you may find these easy, too.

Ballpoint pens require more pressure than felt-tip or marker-type pens. If you are writing quite a lot, you may want to try a felt-tip pen.

Try using foam jackets for pens and pencils. These are designed to slip right onto the pencil and provide a soft, comfortable grip.

The yellow pencil at the top is a mechanical, or drafting, pencil. You never need to sharpen the lead inside. The foam jackets slide onto pens and pencils and give you a better, more comfortable grip.

Wired?

Home computers can certainly be used for storing your day-to-day observations. But just in case there's a power blink or your drive is down, always keep your handwritten field notes.

Some conservationists feel that computers are not environmentally friendly since they use energy and waste paper, especially if you have to reprint something over and over.

Just the Facts

Here is some basic information you'll want to write down in your journal.

Date You'll never remember the exact date if you're on vacation or holiday and a lot of exciting things are happening.

Time Don't just write A.M. or P.M. Some animals, like deer, are crepuscular. That means they are active during dawn or dusk hours.

Weather You can include temperature, wind, humidity, and the sky conditions (clear, over-

The time of day that you observe an animal is important to write down. Most deer are crepuscular. They are active only at dawn or dusk.

Professional wildlife workers and biologists collect additional data in the field. You may want to try to add this information to your own notes.

- latitude and longitude
- elevation, noting low swamps or high mountains, for example
- amount of clouds covering the sky (zero? 50 percent?)
- size or length of animal
- human disturbance of habitat (road-building, construction)

This is a sagebrush and scrubland habitat in Utah. It is hot, dry, and breezy with no large trees.

Dense stands of fir and spruce trees make up this evergreen forest habitat in eastern Canada.

cast, or foggy). Unusual or significant conditions should be noted, such as a drought or severe storms.

Habitat This is the where the animal or plant lives. It's a description of the area where your observations were made. Example: A sand-digging wasp was seen in a habitat of "dry, loose sand at the edge of a soccer field."

Looming clouds may foretell a rain squall. Weather observations can be an important addition to your naturalist's notebook.

Symbols and Signs

You may find it helpful to use a few of the symbols used by scientists when they write technical notes. It speeds up your writing!

♂ This symbol refers to the *male* of any species, anywhere in the world.
♀ This is the symbol for a *female* of any species.
c̄ This means "with."

Here's an example of a quick field note: "Saw a ♀ robin c̄ 3 fledglings."
You can also develop your own shorthand for writing about birds or animals that have long names or that you observe frequently. For example: RWBB is a red-winged blackbird. TV is a turkey vulture.
Just remember to use the same shorthand for that species every time you write about it!

Be Objective

Write down details that you actually see. Don't assume you immediately know what is happening. A human interpretation of what an animal is doing can sometimes be entirely incorrect! You may have to observe an animal several times, before you understand what it is actually doing.

Here's an example. You've just seen a pair of sparrows scratching away in a dusty patch of ground in your garden. They must have scratched the ground bare, right? Maybe not! Birds like to take dust-baths in the summer. This may help to get rid of mites and lice in their feathers. Or, there could be an anthill in that spot, and the sparrows were "anting." That means the birds deliberately squat down near an ant colony, spread their feathers out, and allow the ants to crawl all over their feathers. The ants leave a chemical trail which seems to repel mites and lice. You need to watch the sparrows more closely or on more occasions, to find out what is really going on!

A naturalist stops to write her field notes. Write your notes as soon as you can, since you can easily forget details as the day passes.

TOOLS OF THE TRADE

Binoculars

Binoculars are important for anyone who wants to watch birds or study mammals at a distance. Birdwatchers commonly use 7 × 35, or 7 × 40, binoculars. The number 7 refers to the power, or magnification—the animal you are watching will be enlarged seven times. The 35 means the size, in millimeters (mm), of the big lenses at the other end of the binoculars. You can purchase "binocs" at department stores, camping suppliers, and outdoor sports stores. Ask the salesperson to let you try out the binoculars inside the store so that you can be sure they are clear and sharp. Try looking at an object at the far end of the store.

Buy only binoculars that have *coated optics.* That means that the lenses have a protective coating. There are many expensive brands, but there are also very good brands that are economically priced. Inexpensive, folding binoculars or "compacts" may not be a good choice, however. Their small size makes them hard to hold, and focusing accurately may be difficult.

To get a good view of birds, you need to use binoculars. This is a black-and-white warbler, found in most of eastern and central North America.

Naturalists on a woodland hike are sure to carry binoculars so that they can see details on birds at a distance.

Here's How to Use Them

Your new binoculars will have a focusing dial or a rocker-pad in the center. There will also be a movable ring around the right eyepiece, to adjust the focus for your right eye. Most people do not have perfect 20/20 vision; one eye is often weaker than the other.

Here's how to focus on a distant animal.
1. Keep your eyes directly on the animal.
2. Without looking down, use both hands to bring the binoculars up to your eyes. Keep looking right at the animal.
3. Use your fingers to adjust the central focus, first. Then turn the focusing ring for the right eyepiece.
4. If you look down at your binocs for just one second, you're sure to lose the exact place where the animal was!

Wearing binoculars around your neck for a long time can be uncomfortable. Try attaching a wider strap, like one made for a guitar or camera. A padded, slide-on cover designed as shoulder pads for car seatbelts can also help. Or, just carry your binocs in a field bag or backpack and take them out when you need them.

Use both hands to hold your binoculars steady. Keep your eye on the bird, and don't look down at your binoculars. Focus by feel.

Not Just for Birds

Use your binoculars for other outdoor activities. With them, you can get a better view of sports events, horse shows, or school games. You can also look at distant scenery while on vacation. You'll get a great view of mountains, waterfalls, valleys, and city skylines.

Also, you can go stargazing! Look at constellations and star clusters. Observe the moon at its crescent stage or when it's half-full. A full moon is too bright to look at comfortably.

The magnifying glass with a handle only enlarges an object two times. The two loupes in the center are much more powerful. The magnifying lens at the right is 5× and folds into its own cover.

Binoculars will reveal stunning features and details on the moon. Viewing a half-full or three-quarter-full moon is best.

three times. That's enough magnification for reading small print, but it's *not* enough for nature study. You will need a magnifying lens or loupe that is labeled 5× or 8×, so objects will appear five times or eight times larger.

Warning!

NEVER, EVER try to use binoculars to look at the sun, even during an eclipse. You can cause severe damage to your eyes and even be permanently blinded. Use your binoculars with care and intelligence. Always read the instructions first!

How to Use Magnifiers

Hold the magnifying lens or loupe close to your eye. Hold the object you want to view close to the lens. Move the lens toward your eye or away, or move the object itself closer or farther, until

This small loupe enlarges details fourteen times. Objects must be held quite close to the lens.

Closer and Closer

Magnifying lenses and loupes let you see tiny objects and minute details. Many magnifying "glasses" look like they belong in a Sherlock Holmes story. They have a big, round lens with a straight handle. But most of these lenses only have a magnification of 2× or 3×. That means they can only enlarge an object two times or

you get a clear, sharp view. It takes a little practice and a steady hand.

It's also helpful to close or squint one eye, while looking through the lens with the other eye. If you're indoors, you may need to look at the object under a bright reading light.

Magnifying lenses and loupes are small and lightweight. It's easy to lose or misplace them! Just tie a brightly colored lanyard or cord to your lens, or put a bright sticker on its cover. You'll be able to find it right away, if you drop it on the ground, or leave it on a messy desk.

Caution!

If you focus sunlight directly through your lens onto paper or dry leaves, you could start a tragic fire. Always be careful with your equipment, and use a lens wisely.

Take a Look!

Here are a few things you can inspect closely with your new lens.

Details of an insect: Inspect jaws, legs, or eyes.

The underside of a leaf: You may find fuzz, scales, fine hairs, bright resin dots, or even insect eggs! The leaves of many types of cherry and plum trees have tiny glands near the leaf stem.

Your magnifying glass or loupe is perfect for studying insects. Try looking at the details on jaws, legs, antennae, or eyes.

The underside of this North American bayberry leaf is covered with tiny gold speckles. These are called resin dots and can be seen with a magnifying lens.

The bark of a tree: Get a close-up view of lichens, fungi, and mosses.

Insect antennae: Compare the feathery antennae of a moth to the segmented antennae of a beetle.

Household insects: Discover ants, silverfish, flies, fleas, book lice, and much more. Most homes around the world have insects inside.

A magnifying glass or loupe will give you a close-up view of tiny glands, hairs, or spines on a plant. This bramble leaf is covered with fine hairs.

Field Bags

Hikers and campers almost always carry a field bag or backpack with them. You may want to have a field bag just for nature study that can hold your binoculars, magnifier, sunglasses, notebook, maps, and a granola bar. Many different styles of packs and bags are available to choose from. Here are a few points to consider.

A fanny pack will leave your hands free.

Bags made of nylon weigh less than canvas or leather bags.

Military surplus bags, like paratroopers' bags, are inexpensive and sturdy. They can last a lifetime!

Metal clips, large zipper tabs, and other metal hardware may clatter, jostle, and snag while you are hiking.

You can personalize your field bag by sewing on emblems and patches!

NOTE: If you keep your binoculars in your bag, don't put a can of soda or juice in next to them. Wrap food separately, in leak-proof containers.

Field Guides

Field guides are illustrated manuals used to identify individual species of plants or animals. There are field guides to all sorts of living things: beetles, fish, ferns, land snails, butterflies, orchids, mammals, or birds.

This book is not a technical field guide. It is designed to increase your observation and information-gathering skills, so that you can identify wildlife later, if you want to. With this book, you

Most nature-watchers become interested in studying one particular group of plants or animals. One favorite is the group of club mosses (order Lycopodiales), which is evergreen and can be found year-round.

are learning to look for the clues that will help identify plants and animals: field marks, habitat, and behavior. As you make more and more outdoor observations, you'll probably want to know more about a specific group of animals or plants, like turtles or evergreen trees. *Then* you may want to get a technical field guide.

Trail Guides and Maps

During your hikes and vacations, you may find local trail guides or park maps that illustrate the common plants and animals of the area. Large parks often have information boards, posters, or booklets that describe the wildlife and habitat types. Always take advantage of this information, and use it to try to identify the plants and animals along the trails.

Before you start out on a hike:

Stop to review information so that you can be on the lookout for native animals and wildflowers.

Ask the park ranger or staff naturalist

what you can expect to see.

Ask if there is an observation blind or lookout platform for watching wildlife.

When you return from your hike, ask the park ranger for more details about the plants and animals you observed.

An organized, group wildflower walk is an excellent way to learn about the wildflowers in your area. This is a hepatica flower from the eastern United States.

You Are Not Alone

Around the world many people, young and old, are interested in watching wildlife and finding wildflowers. There are probably groups in your area that organize field trips to observe birds, plants, and insects, or to hike through unique habitats. Group hikes and tours are often given by biologists and naturalists from parks, museums, public gardens, sanctuaries, and arboretums.

The group leader will identify plants and wildlife, and many hikes are free or very inexpensive. You may have to register by phone for some of these tours.

Large parks often have outdoor signs and educational boards to let hikers know what birds or animals have been seen. This sign shows the number of hawks that have been seen on migration.

Special Events

Look for special outdoor events in your area that will help you to learn about your local wildlife or flora.

🦎 Earth Day or May Day talks and tours

🦎 Arbor Day tree plantings and arboretum tours

🦎 Open Farms Day—a chance to visit tree farms, orchards, and fields

🦎 Summer Butterfly Count—Butterflies are caught alive, identified, and then released.

🦎 Christmas Bird Count—Join an organized group for this!

🦎 Hawk Watch—usually held during the autumn migration

🦎 Bird-banding (ringing) demonstrations

On Alert!

Some observation groups have a bird-alert phone number you can call. The taped recording reports the bird species seen during the week. By listening to the taped message, you can learn what birds are common in your area, what species are on migration, and also hear reports of rare birds.

If you are "on-line" you may be able to use your home computer to find a listing or service that provides information on bird sightings, wildlife, or group events.

You can also "tune in" to wildlife by listening to audiocassette tapes. A large variety of tapes are available of songbirds, tropical rain-forest birds, and ravens, and of frogs and toads calling at night. You can listen to tapes of owls hooting or geese honking. Local libraries may have some of these recordings. Listening to these recordings can help you identify the songs and calls of animals in your neighborhood.

A bird-banding, or ringing, demonstration is a great way to learn about the birds that live in your area. You'll get a close-up look at wild birds and find out how biologists track their migration patterns.

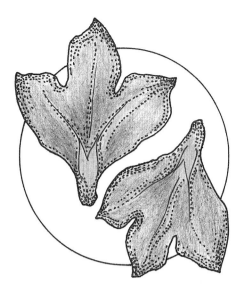

chapter ten

COUNTRY COMFORTS

Get Comfortable!

Hikers, campers, gardeners, and birdwatchers all need to be comfortable while outdoors. Here are some things to consider when choosing clothes for the trail or garden.

Wear loose clothing. You'll need to stretch, reach, and bend to look closely at plants and insects or to use binoculars.

Wear natural fibers, such as cotton or wool. Synthetic clothes, like polypropylene, are recommended for cold environments, but these fabrics and clothes may not be necessary for your activities.

A jacket with large pockets will easily carry trail maps, a snack, and a small notebook.

An overshirt or jacket with large pockets can hold a trail guide, granola bar, sunglasses, scarf, or other personal items.

Pay Attention to Your Feet

Be practical and use common sense when choosing footwear for the field. Men's and boys' dress shoes and office shoes often have smooth soles and are dangerous to wear on a slippery trail or uneven ground. Women's and girls' dress heels, open sandals, and clogs are not a good choice, either. Just imagine trying to walk across a raised wooden boardwalk in heels. You'll get tired fast and risk getting a sprained ankle. The best shoes are those designed specifically for walking and hiking, or running and jogging. Consider whether you need extra ankle support or room for thick, cold-weather socks. Don't wear brand-new shoes on a long hike. Wear them a few times first, for shorter periods, to be sure they will be comfortable for an all-day hike.

Don't buy what you don't need. Rugged, expensive mountain hiking boots with thick soles will only feel heavy and clumsy if you spend most of your time birdwatching on flat ground. However, if you plan a camping trip in rocky, steep terrain, a pair of lightweight canvas sneakers will not give you enough protection.

Sturdy hiking shoes are a necessity for rocky, steep trails.

Special Needs

If you normally wear a sports or elastic support wrap for a knee or ankle problem, wear it or take it with you on a hike. A "short hike" often grows long when you discover something interesting, and you'll be glad you brought the wrap.

If you have a bad back or lower-back pain, walking up a long slope or incline can be difficult and tiring. Consider hiking on flat trails only. If you're planning a trip with friends or with a group, ask ahead of time whether the trails are steep. Try hiking with a walking stick.

Take frequent breaks to give your back, ankle, or knee a rest. Let others in your group know your needs, so no one is surprised when you need to stop and rest.

Many large parks have easy-access ramps and flat pathways for naturalists who use wheelchairs. These trails often wind through different

If you have had an injured knee or back, you might want to choose hiking trails that are flat and even.

habitat areas that you might otherwise never get to experience in your home area. Be sure to read any trail guides that describe plants or birds you're likely to see, and take advantage of the opportunity to study a unique habitat.

Handling Heat and Cold

Hot weather can stop you in your tracks. Loss of body fluids, called *dehydration,* can occur quickly. Don't let yourself get overheated, and don't travel without enough liquids. Here's what to do if you don't feel well and you're overheated.

Let others in your group know you need to take a break.

Get something to drink.

Remove your jacket, or find a lighter shirt to put on.

Get out of the sun.

DON'T move on until you feel better.

Cold weather can also be a problem. Exposure to cold, wet situations can cause *hypothermia,* a dangerous lowering of body temperature. If you plan to be outside in cold weather, take a few easy precautions.

Dress in several layers; you can always remove a layer as you warm up.

Bring along hot cocoa, tea, or other warm drinks.

If you get wet, change into dry clothes as soon as possible.

Keep out of the wind and find a sheltered area.

Much body heat is lost from your head. Wear a hat and use a scarf.

Don't risk getting frostbite just to stay out on the trail a little longer. Know your own limits.

Bring along a canteen filled with water or juice, especially if you're out walking in hot weather.

A comet or other astronomical event can be a once-in-a-lifetime experience. You may need to dress warmly for a cold night or driving wind. Or you'll miss the big event! This is Comet Hyakutake in March 1996.

Most winter sports involve activities that generate body heat. But if you are birdwatching, you'll need to dress more warmly, since you won't be moving around as much.

This is also true for stargazing. If you use binoculars or a telescope at night or if you're watching a lunar eclipse, you'll probably be out in the cold night air for much longer than you expected.

Safety First!

The cold winter months pose unique problems for naturalists. Be sure to play it safe.

Always tell someone where you are going.

Let someone know when you expect to return.

Know your winter trails: Do snow mobiles speed dangerously along the same path you plan to take?

Be sure of your territory. Swamps and ponds may be covered with snow, concealing thin ice!

If you can't keep up with the rest of your group, let them know you need to stop. Don't push yourself.

Don't vow to finish a trail just because everyone else wants to. Nature observation is not a competitive sport. Take your time.

Rest, relax, and review what you've seen so far. Most large parks have benches or lookouts where you can stop to rest.

Your safety, comfort, and well-being are important. Watching wildlife and studying nature should never be uncomfortable.

Always dress warmly for birdwatching in the winter. Bring along an extra scarf and wear gloves.

Refreshment Time

Take a snack or trail food with you on hikes and outings, even if you only expect to be gone a short time. You could run into an unexpected delay traveling or find something interesting, and time will fly! Stash a snack in your jacket pocket, or carry a field bag with a packet of crackers or a box of raisins. Diabetic hikers

A handful of gorp makes a welcome snack on the trail. Create your own mix of nuts, dried fruit, and cereal.

should be sure to take along trail food, so they don't miss out on a scheduled snack or meal.

Many experienced campers like to make their own trail mix, or *gorp*, to take along. Gorp is a dry mixture you can munch by the handful, and it can be carried in any type of small container. Gorp can include any combination of peanuts, cashews, almonds, sunflower seeds, dry cereal, granola, puffed cereal, raisins, or currants, and even chocolate chips or carob chips.

The Battle against Bugs

Don't let insects ruin a day outdoors. Try these tactics to ward off biting insects such as mosquitoes, black flies, and deer flies.

Use the fishermen's trick of putting insect repellent on the top of your hat or cap, and on the visor. Most repellents leave a stain, so you might choose a hat that is only used for buggy trips.

Apply repellent to a small square of cloth and then pin it to your jacket.

Try different types of repellent. Some people insist that only one brand will work for them. Read all the instructions for use.

Spray-on repellents are not a good choice for children, who may get spray in the face. Use a lotion or a roll-on.

Try using a natural, herbal repellent sold in health-food stores.

Wear long-sleeved shorts and long pants. Going on a hike in bug-land wearing a sleeveless shirt will be a miserable experience.

Don't wear perfume. It may only attract insects to you.

Consider wearing a headnet made of mosquito netting. Jackets and pants are also available in netting.

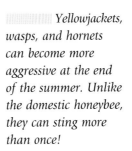

Yellowjackets, wasps, and hornets can become more aggressive at the end of the summer. Unlike the domestic honeybee, they can sting more than once!

Don't Get Stung!

Almost everywhere in the world, there are stinging insects. Hornets, paper wasps, bees, and yellowjackets can all give a painful sting. Here's how you can avoid some unpleasant encounters.

Wear earth-tone colors, such as khaki, sage green, terra-cotta, and ivory. Bright colors and black seem to attract or alarm some stinging insects.

Don't swat or slap at a bee or wasp; this will only make it more likely to sting.

NEVER, EVER drink from an open can of soda pop or juice left outside on a picnic table. Wasps may crawl inside to drink the sweet liquid and then become alarmed when you pick up the can to drink from it. You can get stung on the mouth or face. Pour your drink into an open cup so that you can see the contents.

Apply repellent to your hat visor or hatband to help keep insects away from your face.

Tips on Ticks

Ticks are not insects: they have eight legs instead of an insect's six. The body of a tick looks like a flat, dark sesame seed or watermelon seed. In some areas, ticks carry infectious diseases, so you need to remove them from your skin after a hike.

Tick repellent may be available where you live, but the best precaution is simply to check your clothes, body, and scalp if you have been moving through grasses and shrubs. Ticks found crawling on your skin or clothes can just be flicked away or picked off.

Ticks that are firmly attached should be removed with small forceps or tweezers, placed right at the mouthparts. If you grasp the body instead, you may force fluids from the tick's body into your skin.

Hunters, fishermen, and outdoor workers who move through dense brush and grasses may have many ticks to remove at the end of the day. But if you are hiking along open, clear trails, you probably won't find any, since you haven't brushed against any plants.

This American dog tick is a common pest for some hikers in eastern North America.

Weather Conditions

Light rain or a heavy mist won't stop an experienced birdwatcher from going outdoors. But a sudden thunderstorm or downpour can be dangerous.

Listen to weather reports so that you'll know what to expect. Make plans for another day if the weather is unsettled. Bring along an extra jacket if temperatures are expected to drop at the end of the day.

Wildlife watching and sports don't mix. This hang-glider pilot needs to pay full attention to the safety and operation of his rig.

A Separate Sport

Many outdoor sports are not appropriate for nature observation. Rock climbing, water skiing, white-water rafting, and mountain biking all require sharp attention to safety details. Although these sports may be performed in unique wilderness areas with magnificent views, you'll have little chance to observe or study plants and animals closely. Winter sports, such as snowboarding and skiing, require your full attention for safety so that you avoid having an accident.

chapter eleven

SAVING IT

Keeping Memories on Paper

A personal nature notebook or journal is the best way to record your plant and animal observations. Hikers, birdwatchers, and gardeners can use their notebooks to recall sightings of local wildlife, changes in the environment, and as a reminder of where and when to look for particular birds or wildflowers, year after year. Your handwritten notes will help keep fresh your memory of every bird, mammal, plant, or insect you've seen.

However, if just writing observations isn't enough, or you want to try an additional method of saving your outdoor experiences, here are a few ideas.

Field Drawings and Sketches

Do you think you can't draw a perfect straight line? You don't have to! You don't need to be perfect. You *can* draw and sketch the shells, wildflowers, seedpods, or insects you find outdoors. Don't let anyone tell you that you need lessons or that it's too difficult. You only need to draw the details or parts that will help you remember exactly what something looked like.

Field drawings are a helpful addition to your outdoor journal. Try drawing simple objects first, like large leaves.

Here are a few hints.

Use a whole sheet of paper. Begin by writing in the date, location, habitat, or any other information that seems important.

Try a simple subject. Choose a single leaf or a large flower bud, for instance.

Draw the subject life-size. Line up a leaf with the edge of your paper so that you can see exactly how long or wide it is.

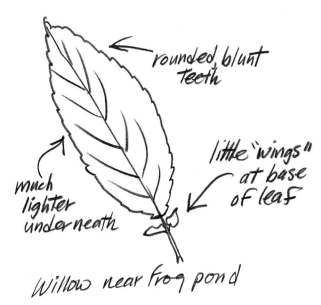

A rough field sketch isn't fine art; it just helps you remember important details.

Compare sizes. Is the leaf as long as your finger? As wide as your palm?

Just draw the outline of a leaf. You can even pick up a fallen leaf and trace its outline.

Look for obvious textures or patterns. You can draw fuzz along a stem, short thorns, or freckles and spots along a twig.

Try to show how the leaf veins are arranged. Are they *parallel*, that is, side-by-side, or do smaller veins branch off from a central main vein, called a *midrib?*

The fuzzy stems and leaves of this alpine poppy are details that can be recorded in your journal or drawn in a field sketch.

Don't spend time trying to shade in a drawing. All you need are simple lines that show size, shape, and texture. Add written notes about colors or details you can't draw.

These field drawings are for your own personal use. Don't be embarrassed by them. They are like a shopping list, using pictures to help you to remember individual details. You won't be showing them to an art teacher!

Outdoor Photography

Most people who spend a lot of time outdoors try their hand at photographing wildflowers, animals, or landscapes. One easy way to begin is by taking photos of scenic views, like farms, mountains, waterfalls, and interesting trees. It is much more difficult to get good shots of birds in flight or of small mammals and insects as they feed and move. No matter what type of camera you use or where you live, you can take better outdoor pictures using these helpful ideas.

Take shots of mosses, lichens, and ferns after a rain or a heavy fog. They look their best when damp!

Take pictures of flowers only when they are freshly opened. A blossom that's been open just a few days already looks faded and worn.

Try taking pictures on an overcast day. Bright days may cause sharp shadows or confusing black areas.

If you are shooting a scenic, panoramic landscape, choose a sunny day with interesting cloud formations.

Be sure that a person in your shot does not appear to have a tree trunk, branch, or telephone pole coming out from his or her head.

Take advantage of the most common birds in your neighborhood. Try seagulls, city pigeons, or park swans. Try to

Wildlife watchers in Australia may have the opportunity to take photos of large birds like this young emu.

stalk close up, and practice getting behavior shots—preening, eating, bathing, or aggressiveness toward other birds.

Take pictures of the same subject on different days and at different times of day. Don't be afraid to experiment.

Take advantage of an artistic still life at the beach. Look for shells, seaweed, or driftwood that have fascinating patterns or textures.

Use any solid support, such as a tree, wall, or bench, to brace yourself or your camera against. That way, the camera will be steady.

Wild ducks and geese sometimes gather at ponds and lakes in large flocks. Use that opportunity to practice composing shots of groups of birds.

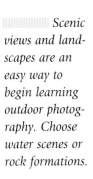

Scenic views and landscapes are an easy way to begin learning outdoor photography. Choose water scenes or rock formations.

If you don't have close-up equipment, try shooting groups or masses of flowers that fill up the frame, like apple blossoms or roses.

Don't be afraid to use several shots (frames) while experimenting to compose a good picture. Remember that professional photographers often use many rolls of film to get just one good shot.

Scenic vacation photographs are an important record of your personal outdoor experiences. Seascapes can be simple but dramatic.

Seaweed and a skate's egg case, called a mermaid's purse, make a good still life to draw or photograph.

This large orchid was photographed without close-up photo equipment. Public gardens and greenhouses are great places to practice your flower shots.

Try This Out

Visit a greenhouse or garden center to practice taking pictures of large flowers. You won't need a close-up lens or other photo equipment if you focus on the largest flowers, such as those of amaryllis, orchids, large roses, and gladioluses. Mounting your camera on a tripod can improve these shots, since the camera will be perfectly steady, allowing you to make a longer exposure.

Don't Be Too Impressed

The seemingly perfect photos you see on magazine covers, in advertisements, or on television often look too good to be true. And they are. Many of these "perfect" shots have been created with electronic imagery, using a computer and electronic scanner to enhance the picture. The colors, lighting, and even the subject itself can be rearranged or re-digitalized by computer to look perfect. Grass can be made to look greener and the sky more blue. A picture of birds in flight with an enormous full moon overhead may actually have been created from two or three different original photographs, with perfect sunset colors added.

So, don't be too impressed by spectacular advertising pictures or magnificent cover photos. Chances are good that computer technology has improved the original shot. You should never feel that your own photographs of wildflowers or wildlife are not valuable. They are authentic and original documents of your personal experience.

And we do want you to know that the nature photos in this book were *not* taken with a digital camera nor were they enhanced by a computer.

Two Tricks

Have you even seen a beautiful photo of a perfect spider's web with morning dew on it? Did you think the photographer really got up early in the morning during just the right weather to capture that image? Maybe not! Many photographers use a spray bottle of water, such as a mister for houseplants, to create dew. Spider's webs and fresh flowers then look sparkling and spectacular.

On a chilly, crisp autumn day, you can also look for large insects, such as grasshoppers, dragonflies, and bumblebees, very early in the morning. It's too cold for these insects to move around yet, so they're likely to stay still while you get your shots. They may even have real dew on them! Get up and out early, dress warmly, and look carefully on flowers and along stems to find these chilled-out models.

Finally, all photographers should respect the environment and refrain from leaving photographic litter outdoors. Film packaging should be disposed of properly. Plastic film containers may be accepted at photo shops for recycling or brought to a recycling station.

Seashells by the Seashore

Travelers and vacationers who visit seashore habitats frequently collect shells, worn beach glass, or attractive pebbles. Often these colorful treasures end up ignored and out of sight in an old shoe box, with any details of where and when they were found long forgotten.

You can easily create an artistic permanent souvenir of your vacation. Simply place the shells or pebbles in a clear plastic or glass container with a label. A small strip of paper with the

Seashells stored in a plastic or glass container will be kept clean and dust-free. Add a label with the date and location your specimens were collected.

exact date and location of your beachcombing adventure is the most important part of your collection. You may never identify all the individual shells, or even want to. But you can keep them clean and dust-free so that you can admire them and recover memories of where and when you found them.

The same seashore specimens can be used at a later date to practice drawing or painting natural objects or for a photographic study. If you revisit the same site years later, you'll be able to compare your older specimens with new ones.

Other natural objects can be stored the same way. An intact, shed snake skin found in your garden or delicate seed pods from a weedy roadside will be kept clean in an attractive jar or container. Remember to label the specimens accurately with the date and location.

Collecting Leaves

If you are hiking or birdwatching in a park or sanctuary, do not collect the leaves of any trees, shrubs, or wildflowers. All plants will be protected.

However, you may find interesting leaves or ferns in your own garden or yard that you'd like to press flat and keep for reference. You may also want to collect a few leaves in the autumn, when they have fallen to the ground. Place the leaves between sheets of newspaper, and set a flat weight on top of the papers. A couple of large books or a book with a rock on top of it is fine. If the weather is dry, the leaves should be dry and pressed flat in several days. In humid weather, this will take longer.

Pressed leaves can be mounted on a card and covered with plastic. Even if you can't identify the leaf, the card should be labeled with the date and location.

To preserve your leaves in good condition for many years, you can construct a leaf card. *Leaf cards* are like a smaller version of a botanist's herbarium specimen. Here's how to do it.

Attach your pressed leaf to a square of heavyweight paper or card stock, using a thin strip of masking tape or paper tape across the leaf stem, called the *petiole*.

A few tiny spots of glue may be necessary to hold a large leaf in place on the card.

Label the card with the date, location, and any comments about its habitat.

For best protection, cut a square of clear acetate or plastic to cover the leaf, and tape it to the card.

You may end up with a considerable collection of leaf cards from many different habitats. Your samples will be valuable for comparing details of textures and veins, and they will be ideal for comparing with illustrations in trail guides or field manuals.

Legal Souvenirs?

Almost every camper, gardener, birdwatcher, or beachcomber has found the molted feather of a bird on the ground. The urge to pick up the feather and attach it to a hat or take it home is strong. But in most areas it is against the law to keep the feathers of migratory birds, without a special license or permit! In the United States and Canada, it is against the law to possess the feathers of a hawk, owl, songbird, or shorebird. The feathers you see on most hats are those of nonmigratory game birds, such as pheasants, grouse, or quail. Many are just dyed chicken feathers.

The nests and eggs of most birds—even when abandoned at the end of the breeding season—

Almost everyone who spends a lot of time outdoors is likely to find a molted feather. This is the tail feather from a male ruffed grouse.

are also illegal to keep. This is to protect many bird species from becoming endangered by commercial, business, or trade groups.

Other natural objects, like fossils, rocks, and minerals, may also be protected by law. Many different wildflower species are likely to be protected. Your best bet is to follow the motto often printed on trail signs or in park guides: "Take only photos; leave only footprints."

In some areas, mineral and fossil collecting may be prohibited. In other places, it is encouraged! Always check regulations first.

INDEX